SOAR ABOVE THE STORMS

Following God From Africa and Across America

DR. MARTIN J. A. RATCLIFFE

Paperback ISBN 978-1-960007-80-3
eBook ISBN 978-1-960007-81-0

Published by

Orison Publishers, Inc.

PO Box 188
Grantham, PA 17027
www.OrisonPublishers.com

Dedication

It is said that an eagle, a bird of prey, soars high above the earth, carried by updrafts and thermals that catch its outspread wings. It rises *above the storms*. In the same way, we can spread our "wings" and rise above life's storms. Isaiah 40:31 says, *"But they that wait upon the Lord shall renew their strength; they shall mount up with wings as eagles; they shall run, and not be weary; and they shall walk, and not faint"* (KJV).

My prayer is that this book will live on to the next generation and even beyond by the Holy Spirit; that people everywhere will be encouraged to put their faith in Christ and follow Him all the days of their lives; that their generation and their children's generation would be drawn to Christ; and that they would know Him as Lord and Savior, the God who is Ever Faithful, Healer, Provider, Redeemer, Deliverer and Miracle Worker—Jesus, the Messiah, the Great I AM, Creator of the universe, my Creator; to Him alone belongs all praise and glory forever and ever. *"Even when I am old and gray, do not forsake me, my God, till I declare your power to the next generation, your mighty acts to all who are to come"* (Psalm 71:18, NIV).

This book is dedicated to God, my Savior; my beloved wife, Shirley Ann; our sons, Timothy James and Thomas Luke; their wives, Carissia and Jerrica; our grandchildren, Archer, Kai, Marek, Carver and Rivers; my siblings, Mary, Brian (Kiey), Liam and their spouses; and *all* readers. "Father, bless each one mightily. Let each know that You are faithful, that You are the Healer, and that You are the Miracle Worker and everything we need. You help us to *soar above the storms*. Amen."

I pray that this book inspires your faith to believe in God for the miraculous and shows you that you can fly like an eagle *above the storms* and fulfill your wonderful God-given destiny. *"From the east I summon a bird of prey; from a far-off land, a man to fulfill my purpose. What I have said, that I will bring about; what I have planned, that I* will do" (Isaiah 46:11, NIV). "Do not fear, for I have redeemed you; I have summoned you by name; you are mine. When you pass through the waters, I will be with you; and when you pass through the rivers, they will not sweep over you. When you walk through the fire, you will not be burned; the flames will not set you ablaze. For I am the Lord your God, the Holy One of Israel, your Savior" (Isaiah 43:1b–3a, NIV).

Special Acknowledgments and Thanks

Thank You, Jesus, for enabling me to write *Soar Above the Storms: Following God From Africa and Across America.* You have shown Yourself faithful throughout my life. Thank You for Your healing, miracles, daily provision, comfort and guidance.

Thank you to my dearest Shirley Ann, my beloved and ever-loving wife, for your faithfulness over the years. Thank you for your insightful initial edits and clarifications for this book and your invaluable *snippets* titled "Shirley's Reflections," those written contributions at the end of each chapter. They add a unique perspective to my story...our story. "*A wife of noble character who can find? She is worth far more than rubies*" (Proverbs 31:10, NIV).

Thank you to my publisher, Marsha; editor, Jeanette; and the Orison team for guarding my story and bringing my dream to fruition. May God continue to bless the work of your hands!

Table of Contents

Map of Africa with Zimbabwe Highlighted

Map of Zimbabwe

Base 802836AI (C00254) 3-02

Key: Town and City Name Changes

New Name (Zimbabwe)	Old Name (Rhodesia)	New Name (Zimbabwe)	Old Name (Rhodesia)
Bulawayo	Bulawayo	Munyati	Umniati
Gweru	Gwelo	Mutare	Umtali
Harare	Salisbury	Somabhula	Somabula
Kwekwe	Que Que	Victoria Falls	Victoria Falls
Masvingo	Fort Victoria	Zvishavane	Shabani

Rhodesia to Zimbabwe

Growing up in British colonial Rhodesia in the 1960s and 1970s was a unique experience, as was the transition of the country to Zimbabwe in 1980. The country was named Rhodesia after Cecil John Rhodes, the wealthy and influential British expansionist who desired to see all lands under British rule.

Established in the early 1890s, Southern Rhodesia (later Rhodesia, in 1964) was a young country that quickly developed towns and cities with excellent roads and rail connections. It had a well-developed mining and farming infrastructure and reportedly exported food to the surrounding nations except for South Africa, which was a highly developed country. The education was British-based and second to none.

The white population in Rhodesia in the mid-1970s was about 270,000, contrasted with about 5,000,000 blacks. (At the time of writing, the white population is about 30,000, and the black population is over 16,000,000.) Whites lived mainly in towns while blacks lived in nearby townships and rural areas. Growing up in Rhodesia in the 1960s and 1970s, I was largely unaware of the growing discontent of some black Africans and the progressive move toward British decolonization in Africa after World War II.

With the introduction of education for blacks and various religious missions providing education, the locals became more educated. They noted how a change in other nations with oppressed populations often happened through a bloody revolution.

Ian Douglas Smith, the first prime minister born in Rhodesia, served as Rhodesia's political leader from 1964 to 1979. He resisted majority rule and Britain's directives to hand over power unconditionally to black majority rule and declared Unilateral Declaration of Independence (UDI) in 1964. This led to enforced sanctions by Britain to pressure the Rhodesian government into compliance and ushered in the protracted bush war for independence from 1964 to 1979.

Two rival political parties, Zimbabwe African National Union (ZANU) led by Robert Mugabe and Zimbabwe African People's

Union (ZAPU) led by Joshua Nkomo, "joined forces" against the Rhodesian government. The Zimbabwe African National Liberation Army (ZANLA) was ZANU's military wing and the Zimbabwe People's Revolutionary Army (ZIPRA) was ZAPU's military wing. Their goal was to destabilize Rhodesia and overthrow the white minority government. China supported ZANLA militarily, and Russia (the Soviet Union) backed ZIPRA. The guerrilla armies were comprised of young African males, who considered themselves to be "freedom fighters," while the white Rhodesian population viewed them as "terrorists."

In December 1979, all political parties met in London at the Lancaster House. They hammered out a political agreement that ostensibly ended the war and handed power to the black majority. Britain regained colonial control and monitored interim elections to ensure that they were free and fair. The country transitioned to Zimbabwe Rhodesia from June 1, 1979, to April 18, 1980, when Zimbabwe gained official independence and was recognized internationally.

My late elementary, secondary and college education was during the Bush War. The war was "somewhere out there" in the early years but landed on our doorstep—literally—in later years!

I was a first-year teacher in 1979 and attempted to capture the essence and *feel* of the Lancaster Agreement and end of the Bush War in the following song that I wrote:

Ceasefire
Fifteen weeks of hard talk, by men who strove for peace
So that our land would be free and endless killing cease

Chorus (after each verse)
Day by day, hour by hour, the battle raged
A battle of guts and staunch determination,
by men who strove to do the best for their nation

Give and take, stop and stall, matters were discussed both big and small
Hopes were raised and then dashed to the ground,
as another flaw in the plan was found

And even while the Big Talk raged,
battle at home was never disengaged
Men were dying every day,
for the cause of freedom, their lives they'd pay

Stopping and starting didn't help the day,
but at last each side had their say
They signed the paper pledging peace,
they said that "now this war will cease"

Over twenty thousand lives were lost, it was a revolution
For the people who were oppressed, sought war as the solution

Men became machinery; they had one goal in mind
To kill the ugly enemy, to their conscience they were blind

At last the paper has been signed, and now there is confusion
As all the people in the land, hope for the illusion

Peace they say is what they want, for all in our land
True peace is what they can have, if for Christ they make a stand

Peace was bought two thousand years ago, by a man on Calvary
Who paid the ultimate sacrifice, so we'd accept it and go free

Prologue

This book is a collection of true stories written to inspire your faith to believe in God for the miraculous. Miracles are not hard; they're *impossible*—without God. But *"with God all things are possible"* (Matthew 19:26b, NKJV). I once saw a sign that said, "We do not believe in miracles; we depend on them." My wife, Shirley, and I depend on miracles. More importantly, we depend on the Miracle Worker, Jesus, for everything. Our faith is not perfect, and we often stumble, but we get back up and keep walking—by faith. We keep believing in God amid good times and crises or storms.

I have heard it said that the Chinese symbol for "crisis" is the same symbol for "opportunity." I am not sure if this is true, but every crisis presents an opportunity to grow in our faith in God; it is another opportunity to prove that His Word is true. It seems that our lives have been marked by crises or storms, but then I see in the Scriptures that we will have trouble. *"These things I have spoken to you, that in Me you may have peace. In the world you will have tribulation; but be of good cheer, I have overcome the world"* (John 16:33, NKJV). The New Catholic Bible puts it this way: *"I have told you this so that in me you may be in peace. In the world you will endure suffering. But take courage! I have overcome the world."*

As I reflect on my life, I see patterns. It seems that each chapter of my life is marked by crises or storms as well as breakthroughs. Researchers identify various life crisis types such as existential, spiritual, identity and so on. Climatologists identify various storm types such as firestorm, squall line and blizzard. The beginning of each chapter identifies a life crisis that aligns with a crisis type and storm type and shows how we can *soar above the storms* by trusting God. The end of each chapter gives subtle clues about another impending storm or crisis. The storms are metaphorical or figurative and not necessarily literal.

The most important crisis or storm to rise above is the existential question about eternity. Why are we here? What is our purpose? Is there a God? Does He love us? How do we get to heaven? How do we find meaning in life? Does God answer prayer? Does He heal? Does He do miracles? Questions abound. To find the answer to these and other questions, we need a divine encounter with the great I AM. Here is my story. It is still being written....

I was raised in war-torn Rhodesia (now Zimbabwe, Africa). My parents emigrated from Ireland when I was very young and then returned to the United Kingdom (UK) where I started school. A few years later they returned to their dream land in Africa. I attended the Hillside Teachers' Training College (TTC) in Bulawayo, Rhodesia (now Zimbabwe), and met Shirley through a mutual friend in my second year. We dated for a while and then went our separate ways (a decision initiated by yours truly). Then one night a friend invited me to a gospel meeting. My life changed. I ran headlong into an old wooden cross, spiritually speaking. The blood was crimson and flowing. My head and heart were splayed open—and *I* died. This book is about my "life after death." "*I have been crucified with Christ and I no longer live, but Christ lives in me. The life I now live in the body, I live by faith in the Son of God, who loved me and gave himself for me*" (Galatians 2:20, NIV).

CHAPTER 1

Adopted By the Father

(1977-1978)

Crisis Faced: Eternity – Heaven or Hell
Crisis: Existential – Life's Meaning
Storm: Heat Burst – Sudden Temperature Increase

Heavenly Encounter
The imploring words of a South African evangelist split the cool evening air. I was riveted in my seat and oblivious to the hundreds of souls gathered in the large city hall in Bulawayo, Rhodesia (now Zimbabwe). "Jesus *suffered* for you!" the evangelist exploded with passionate appeal. "He *died* for you. His back was splayed and His flesh ripped for you!" The evangelist proceeded to name each wound type suffered by Jesus and explain medically what each meant: abrasions, incisions, lacerations, penetrating (puncture) wounds, blunt force trauma and so on. I sat transfixed. I could relate. I had trained with the British Red Cross and was an instructor. I had seen many kinds of wounds.

I was raised as a Catholic and believed in God. I even had a large Jerusalem Bible and had started a Catholic group on the campus of the teachers' college I was attending. But I had never heard the gospel preached so passionately. Indeed, I had never "heard" the gospel made as alive and real and confrontational as this evangelist made it. It was as though God was speaking to me personally, like I was the only person in the room. He had my full and undivided attention. Then a singer (Gwen Murrey) sang "Adopted" from her album "All My Riches" (1976). It was an upbeat catchy gospel song about the Father's love and how He adopted us as His children and redeemed us with His blood. The singer then spoke briefly about her "Daddy." I had never heard our heavenly Father referred to as "Daddy." This was foreign to me, but I could feel His presence and love through that song and this singer and the gospel message. My heart ached for more. I so desperately wanted to meet this Jesus who had borne my sins and sicknesses and sorrows.

The evangelist continued his sermon. The atmosphere was electric. My heart was thumping in my chest. "Perhaps you are still in your sins tonight," he said. "You've never made a stand for Christ. He laid down His life for you. His heart was literally torn in two with blood and water gushing out as evidence when a soldier pierced His side with a spear. What more could He give—the sinless Lamb of God?" The evangelist then listed types of sinners such as murderers, thieves, liars, adulterers, swindlers and the like. I did not "fit" into any of these "sin" categories. Finally, the evangelist said, "Perhaps you are in the most difficult sin category. You are a religious person. You believe in Jesus, but you've never publicly acknowledged Him as your Lord and Savior. You've never made a public *stand* for Christ." He continued, "In Matthew chapter 10 verses 32 and 33, Jesus said, '*Whoever acknowledges me before others, I will also acknowledge before my Father in heaven. But whoever disowns me before others, I will disown before my Father in heaven*' [NIV]. Tonight is your night. Raise your hand if you would like to make a stand for Christ and give Him your life."

An internal battle raged. This was my moment of inner crisis. I knew God was speaking directly to me through the singer and evangelist. My heart was pounding with conviction and about to burst open. But I could not raise my hand. I wasn't resisting raising my hand; I just couldn't send it vertically. I slowly yielded control of my will to Jesus. Then, almost imperceptibly, as though someone had tied a dozen helium balloons around the index finger of my right hand, my arm slowly floated upward and remained pointing toward heaven. The evangelist then challenged those who had raised their hands to come forward so he could pray for us.

I stood, moved into the center aisle, and then shuffled to the platform where the evangelist stood beckoning. I was twenty years old with scruffy beard growth, but only one thing mattered. I had given my life to Christ and was making a stand for the One who'd given everything for me. Once at the front of the hall, I was directed to stand in front of the huge stage with others who had come forward. In my peripheral vision, I caught sight of Shirley, a young lady I had dated less than a year prior.

We had met through a mutual friend and started dating. We even prayed together with me leading in prayer. I thought I was a Christian, but I did not have a "born again" relationship with my heavenly Father through Christ. I'd never made a public stand for Christ. It was this "feeling" of something being different between us that led me to listen to counsel from my college buddies. I stopped dating Shirley but remained "friends."

The evangelist's beckoning appeal suddenly caught my attention, and I refocused on him. "Pray this prayer with me if you are serious about following Christ." I prayed along with the evangelist. "Father, forgive me for my sins. I am so sorry. Thank You for sending Your Son, Jesus Christ, to pay the debt for my sin that no one else could pay. Thank You for the blood of Jesus that washes away my sin. I ask You to come into my life and be my Lord and Savior. I promise to follow You for the rest of my life. I completely surrender to Your will. Amen."

I awoke the next morning with a powerful feeling of excitement stirring in my gut. It seemed that an enormous weight had been lifted, and indeed it had. The dead, leaden weight of sin had been removed, and it was as though I floated to classes on campus three feet above the ground. I was filled with joy and love. My friends noticed a difference. I was more generous with my possessions and car. My desire for God and the things of God increased.

Shortly after my encounter with God, I went to Shirley's apartment and announced, "I now know what you have. I, too, have accepted Christ." She was ecstatic. We continued to be "just friends," however. My decision to follow Christ was the most pivotal ever and set the course of my entire life.

Hiking from Harare to Cape Town

My college friend Mike and I decided to hike to Cape Town and ascend Table Mountain. This was Christmas 1977. We had both completed three years at the Teachers' College in Bulawayo, Rhodesia (now Zimbabwe). We had been among the select few accepted into the Bachelor of Education degree program at the University of Rhodesia (now Zimbabwe). Mike lived in Salisbury (now Harare), and I lived in Fort Victoria (now Masvingo). This was during the height of the Bush War in Rhodesia. People were encouraged to drive in convoys between cities, especially out-of-the-way cities. The convoys included a military escort and could number several hundred vehicles. They were also ideal means for hitchhiking.

Mike hitchhiked from Salisbury to my home in Fort Victoria. We both hitchhiked from Fort Victoria to Johannesburg, several hundred miles away in South Africa. We spent a month traversing South Africa, visiting friends, hiking through the Transkei, and camping out on the side of the road at the foothills of the Drakensberg Mountain range. I recall praying one morning and reading Psalm 121. "*I lift up my eyes to the hills—from whence comes my help? My help comes from the Lord, who made heaven and earth*" (Psalm 121:1–2, NKJV). Several exciting adventures later we made it to the top of Table Mountain in Cape Town.

We had booked a train ticket (compliments of my dad, who worked on the Rhodesia Railways) from Cape Town to Pretoria. At that point, we had a dollar and change between us for the three-day journey back to Rhodesia.

Karate Punch

Once college finished, I moved to the capital city of Salisbury (now Harare) to attend the University of Rhodesia (now Zimbabwe). My thirst for God and His Word continued. I held spiritual conversations with the priest and nuns at Saint Michael's School where I exchanged oversight duties for board and lodging. Strangely, the African priest never understood my experience of coming to Christ. I also joined an off-campus Bible study composed of university students and professors. I distinctly remember one science professor's powerful analogy to defeat Darwin's theory of evolution. He said, "If I had all the pieces of a watch at hand and set an explosive under them, what would be the chance of all the pieces coming together in perfect harmony as a completed working watch?" This analogy enabled me to grasp the lunacy of evolution. Creator God made the universe with intention and design.

I had started karate training after high school graduation, continued at the Teachers' College in Bulawayo, and then trained in three different styles in the capital city of Harare. I was also the instructor at one dojo in the powerful but "rigid" Japanese style of Shotokan. One evening, I sparred with Shukokai instructor Graham at his dojo. He had been runner-up in the world championships in the fluid Shukokai style. I did not fancy my chances of scoring any points but gave it my best shot. I tried to fake him out and foot-sweep him. However, he was lightning-fast, and he swept me instead. This caused me to fall toward his snap-like punch that connected with my right eye orbit. I collapsed like a deck of cards and knew I had been hit hard. My head pounded from the concussion, and I quickly developed a tennis ball-sized contusion.

Talk about timing…Shirley had traveled from her hometown in Bulawayo and asked me to accompany her to a friend's wedding. I had accepted. The wedding was the day after my eye encountered Graham's explosive punch. Shirley insisted on my going to the hospital after the wedding. I resisted at first but then yielded to her good sense. After all, she had done some nursing. The doctor X-rayed my eye and showed me where my orbit had been fractured. My facial bone below my eye was pushed in and down. I was offered plastic surgery for cosmetic purposes. I did not consider myself to have movie star good looks, so I declined the surgery. I noticed that the top teeth on my right side were "numb." I could also still feel the bony nodule where the break occurred in my orbit. To this day (many years later), my teeth are still somewhat numb, and I can still feel the orbit nodule.

I'd received a "wake-up" punch but continued to train harder than ever in each of the karate styles. I even trained on weekends. One day several months later, I walked to the front of the dojo in my own style and was about to begin class. I was dressed in my white gi and brown belt. Suddenly I felt God's tangible presence and sensed the Holy Spirit calling me to lay karate aside. The urge was so strong that I knew it was the Holy Spirit. Those who knew me knew that "Marty loved karate" and that he'd never make such a decision on his own. But the Holy Spirit insisted, and I yielded. The class was stunned when I told them I would no longer be their instructor. I finally received God's memo about karate. It was a wrong priority in my life, and it had to go, at least for now.

I graduated from the university at the end of the year with my bachelor's degree in education and moved to an asbestos-mining town and my first full-time teaching position. The Bush War was in full swing. There were many life lessons still to be learned. God was helping me to *soar above the storms*. Still, I could sense intense heat ahead....

Shirley's Reflections

Martin and I dated for six months before he broke up with me when he dropped me off at home one night. I was very upset, but I told him that if that was what he wanted, I was fine with it. I went upstairs to bed sobbing my heart out. I kept in touch for birthdays and Christmas and Easter, and occasionally I asked him to accompany me to a special event. He politely obliged but was no longer interested in me. I was Martin's first, last, but *not* only girlfriend.

CHAPTER 2
War Miracles
(1979-1980)

Crisis Faced: Life and Death – Annihilation
Crisis: Physical – Survival
Storm: Firestorm – Intense Heat from a Large Fire

Elections Call-Up

I was summoned by the local Shabani (now Zvishavane) town council and appointed as the Presiding Officer in charge of elections at a rural polling station. The national elections were scheduled during the four-week school holidays. I would be away for the next eight days for the elections. This was my civic duty as a teacher. I was not trained as a soldier; I was a civilian—a teacher. A first-year teacher.

My church friend Desmond oversaw the logistics of the elections locally. He was retirement age but still active in the community and our local church. When I arrived at his office, he informed me that I would be setting up a polling station way out in the bush and would have a military escort and protection. What he didn't tell me was that this was the *second hottest* guerrilla-terrorist area in the country. He also informed me that I would not be issued a weapon since the British were monitoring the elections to make sure they were free and fair. I could not see myself going into the thick of the African bush *in the middle of the*

Bush War without a weapon, so I strongly objected. Desmond pushed back at first but finally relented and issued me a G3 weapon and strict instructions to keep it from plain view during daylight. I agreed. I was not issued a camouflage uniform, but I dressed in khaki pants and an olive-green sweater as a substitute.

On Sunday noon, I arrived at the expansive local grass airfield and joined an ethnically mixed group of army and police reservists, including blacks, whites and Indians, on the back of a large open military truck. Several other trucks were present along with a minesweeper vehicle with a V-shaped undercarriage designed to deflect road mine explosions. I was unacquainted with the G3 and asked the sergeant next to me to show me the safety catch. He looked at me incredulously but showed me how to activate the safety mechanism. Later that evening, when we had reached our destination and set up camp, he did not accept my volunteering to stand guard duty. I think I know why. But I was willing to do my part. Soon we were rumbling out of town with lap belts securely fastened.

Our convoy headed north along a main road that paralleled a range of blue hills in the distance. It was smooth at first. We then turned east off the main road onto a dirt road and continued our bumpier trek. Initially the trip was uneventful, but then we stopped suddenly. All was still. The azure sky above was deceptively calm. Nobody spoke. Several minutes later we trundled over metal supports laid across a ditch. Guerrilla-terrorists were expecting us.

We arrived at our bush destination by late afternoon. We set up camp in a circular fashion, about forty yards in diameter, in the middle of the wooded outcrop that was slightly elevated above the surrounding wooded African bush. To the west was a small brick building with a padlock on the door. This building was designated as the polling station. The tea chest-size polling boxes were placed safely out of sight. Beyond the building was a narrow footpath that we later discovered led to a river about a third of a mile away. Several soldiers were dispatched to conduct a 360° security perimeter check about a hundred yards from camp. They also set up claymore anti-personnel mines with trip wires to aid in alerting us to enemy insurgents and hopefully act as a deterrent.

We were encouraged to "zero" in our weapons by firing at a makeshift target. I tried out my G3. It was deadly accurate. Furthermore, the guerrilla-terrorists now knew we were a force to be reckoned with. I "messed" with several police reservists and used the metal shovel I'd brought to help carve out a shallow trench. However, it was more like a shallow depression than a trench as the ground was hard and rocky. It would barely protect us from enemy fire and only if we were completely prostrate in pancake fashion. The sergeant crept stealthily around the perimeter and assigned each of us an "arc of fire." This was to minimize "friendly fire" and increase the chances of striking the enemy. A few minutes later, he "barked" a barely audible husky command. "Stand to." Instinctively, I thought he meant to stand upright, but I noticed how others made themselves invisible with the dirt and just as silent.

Dusk fell like a dead paratrooper descending silently into an ember-red night sky. The Msasa trees were exquisitely silhouetted against the glowing orange-red canvas. Soon it was inky black. All was deathly still.

Sleep did not come easily. I lay on my back and looked up at the stars through the silver leaves of Msasa trees. I then peered through the blackness of night at the base of the trees. A full moon was cresting the horizon silently, and eerie shadows played tricks with my mind. Were the guards alert? Was that a movement? The cool night air was as still as though it was frozen in time. I controlled my breathing—and prayed silently. "Father, thank You for Your peace and angelic protection tonight. I trust You completely, whatever the night should bring. If this is my last night, I am ready to meet You, dear Jesus. Thank You for Your precious Holy Spirit's calm and reassurance. Amen." "*And the peace of God, which transcends all understanding, will guard your hearts and your minds in Christ Jesus*" (Philippians 4:7, NIV).

I had recently broken my left thumb playing rugby for the local asbestos mine's team. I'd strong-armed a would-be wing tackler with a stiff karate-like chop one time too often, and he had read my movement and spun me around violently, cartwheeling me into the hard green dirt rugby field surface. My thumb jutted forward instead of backward. Pain exploded through my body. However, I refused to let the team down and hastily immobilized my thumb with my handkerchief and resumed my position on the left wing. Later I saw a doctor who placed a shiny aluminum splint around my thumb. Now I wondered if this aluminum splint would glisten in the moonlit night and provide a welcome target for guerrilla-terrorist fire. I had no way of bending it out of the way. I prayed some more.

Almost imperceptibly, I slipped into sleep as though floating on tranquil waters. I barely submerged beneath sleep's surface. My mind was fully alert. I was hyper-vigilant, but my body was in emergency sleep mode. Time passed…7:30 p.m.…8:00 p.m.…9:00 p.m.…10:00 p.m. The night was young. I lay motionless on my back on top of my sleeping bag on the rocky surface. To my right at the position of three o'clock was a rocket launcher armed and dangerous. Slightly above it at the position of one o'clock, the dreaded MAG heavy-duty machine gun was dug in and ready. At twelve o'clock on the camp perimeter was one of the night guards. Each guard did a three-hour stint of watching for guerrilla-terrorists.

Suddenly the night stillness was shattered into a million pieces. A burst of gunfire sent red tracers overhead. I instinctively pancaked onto my front by hastily hinging to my right. Unfortunately, the police reservist next to me did the same, except he turned to his left, and we collided midway. The other police reservists were equally disorganized. Looking back, this was one of our "funnier" moments, but nothing was amusing about the chaos at the time. Our failure to plan could have resulted in our deaths. Silence. Moments ticked by and seemed like hours. I controlled my breathing. In. Out. In. Out. Slowly. Quietly. There was no way of knowing who the gunfire was from. Then the sergeant made the rounds inside the security perimeter. He crept stealthily like a black cat.

"It was one of our guards. He thought he saw movement in the shadows, but it was only a cow," he whispered.

I exhaled silently. There was no doubt now that the guerrilla-terrorists knew exactly where we were if they had ever doubted. I whispered to the reservists that we should all hinge to the right to avoid crashing into each other. They agreed. We had a plan.

An hour later, the guard opened fire again. This time the reservists and I hinged to the right; semi-automatic weapons poised at the ready in our designated arc of fire. Then silence. Later in the night, the guard opened fire again. This time the MAG gunner joined in the action with thunderous and deadly boom, boom, boom, boom gunfire lighting up the night sky. So much for any more shut-eye. I later discovered that the MAG gunner had fired as a deterrent to any would-be assassins coming our way.

Dawn lit up the African sky in brilliant hues of red and orange. Soon the sun was cresting the treetops. Controlled cooking fires were lit and pre-made Military Ration Meals (MREs) called "Ratpacks" were opened. The food was welcome, and I thought it was quite tasty. Anything with baked beans was tasty to me. Later in the morning, I set up the polling station in the nearby secured building. There was no key to unlock the padlocked door, so one soldier offered to kick the door open. It didn't work. Then I offered to try a karate side thrust kick. The door flew open, and we had access to the building.

Foldable voting booths were opened and set upright in an organized fashion inside the single-room building. Secrecy in voting was pivotal. Ballots and markers were ready. Voters would simply place an X next to the name and picture of the person they wanted to serve as president of the new country transitioning from Rhodesia to Zimbabwe Rhodesia in mid-1979. (Zimbabwe Rhodesia was not recognized internationally, however. Less than a year later, the country further transitioned to Zimbabwe and was recognized internationally.) A few volunteer soldiers and I set up two tables with folding chairs for "helpers." The outside arrangement allowed voters to line up and then dip their fingers in an invisible liquid. Intending voters would then pass their fingers under an ultraviolet light. If their fingers turned purple, we knew they had already voted and would not be permitted to vote again.

The soldiers and police reservists took turns casting their votes on the first election day. I voted, too. However, locals in the area stayed put as they were fearful of the guerrilla-terrorists and their threats.

I walked back across a dirt road to our camp and found my shovel. I decided to dig a trench between the rocket launcher and MAG gunner—with the sergeant's permission. This would alleviate the load in our makeshift saucer-shallow hollow and perhaps afford better protection from enemy gunfire. Digging was slow going, and soon I was perspiring heavily. The jolting of the metal shovel against hard dirt and rocks sent electric spasms of pain through my broken thumb and up my left arm. But I was determined to "dig in" before nightfall. One of the African soldiers nearby saw me struggling and offered to help. I gratefully accepted his offer. Finally, the trench was finished. It was about twenty inches deep in the front half and eighteen inches deep in the back half owing to an impenetrable larger rock mass. Dirt and rock mounds surrounded the trench. I was hoping the "sandbag effect" would stop AK-47 rounds, but I was not about to stake my life on that and was determined to stay as earthbound as possible should enemy fire come my way. I gladly exchanged sleep discomfort for the perceived notion of being less of a target. I dug a "square" three-foot hole at the bottom of my trench and hid the empty ballot box with leafy tree coverings.

Dusk fell. Another moonlit night arrived. Deafening silence permeated. I slowly drifted into a hyper-vigilant shallow sleep and then sank a little further beneath the twilight sleep zone. Suddenly, I shot upright, sitting straight, an easy target for the enemy. I could hear myself call out, "That's academic!" And then I laid down and continued "sleeping." I heard the next morning that I had scared the "bejeebers" out of the guards. No more talking dreams after that.

Voting numbers increased on Tuesday and Wednesday as the military reached out and escorted locals to the bush polling station so they could vote safely. Most folded their ballot and slid it through the thin slit in the top of the tea chest ballot box with a little coaxing from helpers. Others tore their ballot in half or shredded it in several pieces to fit the ballot through the narrow slit. They had never participated in "free and fair" elections, and some were quite bewildered by the proceedings.

Sunshiny clear skies persisted throughout the week. Warm days and azure skies were had during the day. Silky black night canvases with sparkling starlike diamonds covered the evening sky with silver beams of moonlight shooting through the leafy acacias. Despite the high alert of danger, I experienced God's overwhelming peace. I knew that if I died, I would join God in glory and be with Him forever. I was secure in my faith and could sense His presence.

There are no bathrooms out in the bush. Military personnel navigate this without a thought, but this was a new experience for me. I was also not used to having an armed escort with me when attempting to do my business outside the camp. Ten days after departing the eight-day election camp, a doctor prescribed a laxative. Eighteen days without waste elimination was a record for me and could have had serious consequences.

Early each morning before sunrise, several soldiers would depart from camp into the African bush and "do a 360." They would move silently in single file about a quarter of a mile from camp and then maneuver through the trees and bush just as dawn was breaking. They would complete a 360° canvas of the area to roust out any guerrilla-terrorists. The first few days were uneventful. Thursday *was* eventful.

We were rousing and preparing for the day. The early morning telltale silver rays of dawn stretched its long fingers across another cloudless sky. Today would undoubtedly be the strongest showing of locals at the makeshift polling station. Thud! Thud! Thud! Brief silence. Thud! Thud! Thud! Brief silence. More thuds. More silence. More thuds. Silence. The morning calm was shattered like a rock hurled through a church's stained-glass window. We instantly assumed our firing positions and waited with breath abated. Breathe in. Breathe out. Focus. Pray. Wait. Finally, the sergeant received a radio message from the soldiers conducting the 360. They had flushed out the supposed guerrilla-terrorists out of the tall bush grass. They had apparently tried to run away and were shot. Seconds rolled into minutes. Time dragged on.

I assumed my duties at the polling station with little hope of locals coming to cast their votes. I wasn't disappointed. Around midmorning I heard a pitiful, mournful sound coming from the camp. What could it be? The wailing continued unabated. Finally, I closed up shop and wandered over to the camp to see what was happening. I signaled the medic and asked if I could see what was happening. He ushered me over to a flatbed military truck. I found a young African woman about eighteen years old lying on her back, whimpering and wailing forlornly. Loudly. She was in obvious, excruciating pain. The medic explained that she had been severely wounded when mistaken for a guerrilla-terrorist. I later found out that the supposed guerrilla-terrorists had been frightened locals hiding in the fields and bush.

The teen's lower legs were shattered, disfigured and bloody. She had also been shot in the pelvis, the bullets exiting the abdomen with gaping wounds. I had previously spoken to the African medic and told him

I was British Red Cross-trained and able to offer some help in emergencies. I asked him what he had done. He said nothing. Her veins had collapsed. He could not give her an IV. There was nothing he could do. I wondered if we could try the veins in the neck. However, I was not trained in the art of intravenous injections, and the medic was resigned to her impending death. I called for someone to bring me a blanket. It was cold in the shade, and this young girl was shivering in deep shock. I mounted the flatbed and gently covered the teen. Her breathing was labored. The wailing continued. And then the teen started calling loudly in desperation over and over. I asked the African medic what she was saying. He said, "She is calling for her mother."

I did all I could do. All I could do was try to keep her comfortable and wait. I felt helpless. Choppers were not allowed in the area because of the suspected guerrilla-terrorist presence. Vehicles could not traverse the roads back to my hometown and a hospital two hours away because of the possibility of landmines. A mobile minesweeper would need to go ahead of us, carefully checking for subterranean explosive devices. The teen suddenly took a deep breath and slowly exhaled. It sounded like a hollow cardboard box exhaling. Silence. The wailing stopped. The heaving chest failed to rise again. She had let go of this life. She lay motionless. Dead. I stared for a few moments. At least she was no longer in pain. Death seemed so surreal. I had desperately wanted to save this teen's life, but this was Africa, and we were in the middle of the Bush War.

The following day I joined several soldiers in a single file "march" through the bush toward the river. I was careful to have my G3 pointing to the left side at a 45° angle. I relied heavily on hearing in my right ear since mumps had caused nerve deafness in my left ear on my thirteenth birthday. I was vigilant and rotated my head from left to right like a slowly oscillating fan. This would give me the best chance of picking up any unusual sounds. In reflection, I could have been a liability for the others.

About twenty minutes later we arrived at the banks of a wide river flowing lazily in a ravine. Smooth granite boulders lay like sleeping elephants along the banks. We took turns slowly creeping down to the river's edge and quickly bathing. The rest of us stood guard in the shadows of the acacia trees. In truth, those bathing in the river were any sniper's delight on the ridge across the river. After several days of not bathing, the risk seemed worth it, and the cool waters were refreshing. I didn't give the dreaded water-borne bilharzia disease a second thought. Strange, since I was usually careful to avoid rivers and dams.

Sunday morning rolled around, and we packed up camp. A little later, the camouflaged open-back military vehicles convoyed behind the minesweeper. The ballot boxes were secured beside me. We were on our way home. Mission accomplished. The peace of God was still guarding my heart. "*Peace I leave with you; my peace I give you. I do not give to you as the world gives. Do not let your hearts be troubled and do not be afraid*" (John 14:27, NIV).

Under Attack

I was still in my first year of teaching in a small asbestos mining town just over an hour by car from where my parents lived in Rhodesia (now Zimbabwe), southern Africa. The Bush War was at its peak, and stringent curfews had been advised for travelers. People commuted between towns only between 8:00 a.m. and 4:00 p.m. and almost always with a military escort.

I lived in the "men's mess," a house designated for single male teachers. The brick house with the typical gray asbestos roof was on the outskirts of town on a side road opposite a high wooded hill with a reservoir on top. A main road ran between my home and the hill. This location was known as "Ambush Alley" since "freedom fighter" guerrilla-terrorists had a distinct advantage and could use the hill to launch rocket attacks against the town.

One day I was visiting my parents in their hometown of Fort Victoria (now Masvingo). I traveled without the customary military escort (a police pickup with a mounted machine gun manned by a trained shooter hidden behind a V-shaped protective steel body shield with a narrow slit to see through). It was not easy to schedule around escorts, and I had to return the following day to play community cricket.

The trip to my parents' home was uneventful, as was the return trip on Saturday morning. But when I returned, I heard that there had been a firefight that various military and police groups stationed in the area had participated in. Apparently one military group heard gunfire and thought they were under attack. They returned fire. This set off a firestorm from another military group, and so on. The jittery nerves of the police and military had been stretched thin, and the slightest enemy "provocation" or perceived provocation was met with chaotic resistance. There was no guerrilla-terrorist attack. But I had missed the fireworks, which I heard were spectacular. We still played our cricket match despite the previous night's firestorm.

On another night, I heard several gunshots. Boom! Boom! Boom! I peered through the lattice window of the front door and then opened it. Silence. I waited. My breathing was slow and controlled, but my heart was pounding. Was this the night the enemy would attack? The sounds of silence were deafening. A few minutes later there was another gunfire volley. This time I could see red tracers ripping through the black night sky. I had been called up to do military service but was needed as an elementary classroom teacher. My limited experience with guns involved shooting a .22 rifle once as a ten-year-old, "zeroing" a G3 rifle using a couple of rounds, and shooting a few rounds with my semi-automatic LPD (Rhuzi) machine gun just to make sure I knew how to use it. However, it was no match for the guerrilla-terrorists' AK-47 machine guns. I stood transfixed for a moment, then decided to go inside just in case.

Rocket-Propelled Grenade (RPG) Home Attack

I remember yet another night when the guerrilla-terrorists attacked my parents' home. Ring. Ring. Ring. I was startled by the early morning phone call. "Who could be calling at this hour?" I asked myself groggily as I stumbled out of bed and toward the phone in the hallway. It was August 1, 1979. I was still in my first year of teaching.

"Hello," I mumbled.

"Martin, we've been hit by terrorists." The all-familiar voice of my Irish mother resounded. "We're not hurt. I called because I didn't want you to worry if you heard about it over a newsflash."

I listened to the seemingly calm voice of my mother, but I was not convinced that all was well. I put the phone down slowly and sat in stony silence. It was 5:00 a.m.

A rush of emotions flooded my soul, and anger began to rise in me like a rocket rising from its launching pad. I knew I had to travel home immediately to see how everyone was for myself. With one leg in a cast from a recent rugby game, mobility was awkward at best. I would have to struggle with the Datsun's stick shift and use the rubberized heel of my cast to press against the clutch. This was not going to be a picnic. I quickly dressed, slung my semi-automatic Uzi-like LPD machine gun over my shoulder, and headed for the car. All was still—too still, it seemed. The heavens hung pregnant with silver stars as though waiting for something to burst forth.

The engine roared to life and after a jolting start, I started toward my parents' home. My foot was like lead against the accelerator. The indicator on the speedometer climbed rapidly and then stuck against the extreme right: 40, 50, 60, 80, 100, 120, 140, 160 km/h. It continued to climb. I pushed my new Datsun over the limit blindly into the thick darkness against all reason, ignoring the "safety" curfew and unshaken by the likelihood of a guerrilla-terrorist attack enroute or the chance that I might hit a landmine. Neither was I considering the possibility of meeting one of the many farm animals that frequently meandered across the road. My mind was frozen in time and single-mindedly focused on the welfare of my parents and siblings. What if they had been injured or killed? A myriad of anxious and angry thoughts raced through my mind.

About twenty miles out on this two-way highway, my car lights picked up a disturbance in the tarred road. By the time I had processed what this might be, I was on top of it. I felt a slight ripple in the tires and continued my journey at breakneck speed. It wasn't until the return trip that I realized that I had crossed a three-foot-wide and one-and-a-half foot-deep trench dug by guerrilla-terrorists designed to slow one down—permanently. A mile farther down the road, a heavy cement road sign pole had been uprooted and lay across the median. This was another ploy of the guerrilla-terrorists to slow down unsuspecting victims. I did not have time to slow down, but incredibly, my steering wheel moved slightly to the left, and I miraculously avoided the deadly pole. For the second time in less than a minute, I cheated death. In a record thirty-five minutes, I had traversed the sixty-five-mile, door-to-door commute along a winding two-way road in the early morning hours and was turning down the road where I'd grown up. Police had cordoned off the area, however, and would not allow me through at first.

The house next door to my parents' was billowing black smoke. It had been completely razed to the ground. My parents' home was still standing, but the roof was partially missing. On seeing my family, relief flooded in like a mighty torrent. Despite the damage to the house, all was well on the home front, even though they were badly shaken. Once inside, I gazed through the gaping hole overhead into the azure expanse suspended above where a Russian-made RPG anti-tank grenade had exploded in the early morning hours. Also, a stick grenade exploded near the house and shattered windows. The guerrilla-terrorists had opened fire from behind the park hedge across the road.

The concussion from the incredible explosion had blown my mom out of bed so that she landed squarely on her knees on the red polished cement floor. (Her knees were badly bruised for months.) Later that morning she joked with a reporter, telling him, "I always said it would take a bomb to get me out of bed early in the morning." *Way to go, Mom!*

The aroma of sizzling eggs, bacon, toast and freshly made tea filled the gunpowder-tainted air. Dad's breakfast was always tops, and he was not about to let this incident interfere with home life.

Years later, my "baby" brother Liam told me that a tree branch in front of my parents' window had deflected one of the RPG anti-tank grenades, which fortunately did not explode. I hate to think of the outcome had this "divine" intervention not occurred. God's angels were certainly at work. This guerrilla-terrorist attack shook the community and was still a topic of conversation more than forty years later when my two surviving siblings and my wife and I returned for a school reunion.

I drove back to my teaching post at a more sedate pace. I knew for sure that within the space of just a few hours, my family had escaped death, including myself—twice. I could sense the presence of the Lord saying, "*Fear not, for I am with you…*" (Isaiah 41:10, NKJV). I knew that regardless of what happened next, I was in the hands of God.

Brightlighting

Shabani (now Zvishavane) is an asbestos mining town surrounded by hills. There is no snow in Zimbabwe, but "asbestos" flakes would fall from the sky like snow occasionally. I taught in the local "primary" (elementary) school and became fully immersed in all aspects of the school.

I was twenty-two years old at my first assigned teaching post. I produced two plays, coached students in various sports, and was active in local sports life, particularly tennis, squash (like racquetball), cricket and rugby. I also went horseback riding on the weekends. I even taught karate for a while, until God convicted me through His Word. "*As a dog returns to its vomit, so fools repeat their folly*" (Proverbs 26:11, NIV). I repented and stopped. Again. On occasion, I would "brightlight"—or act as an armed guard—for farmers who needed to travel. Having an active armed presence on farms served as a deterrent to guerrilla-terrorists who may think twice before attacking.

One day I was stranded on a dirt road out in the bush about twenty miles from my town. I was driving without an armed escort. The road had come to a fork, and I was not sure which way to turn to reach my friend Peter's farm. I met Peter (not his real name) at a local church I was attending. He was several years older than I and the manager of a large area farm. I opened the door of my white Datsun, my semi-automatic machine gun slung lazily over my shoulder, just in case, when I noticed the dust cloud of an approaching pickup truck.

The pickup pulled over to the side of the road and out stepped a neighboring farmer, Mr. Richardson (not his real name). He was an older man. We became acquainted, and he quickly pointed me toward Peter's farm. I explained that I was visiting Peter since he had asked me to brightlight his farm, and I needed to become familiar with the layout and expectations. "Do you brightlight for others?" he inquired. I considered his proposition, and he hired me on the spot to come and brightlight on his farm for three weeks, which coincided with my upcoming school winter break. This was dangerous work. Mr. Richardson had already been attacked by guerrilla-terrorists on a couple of occasions. (Farm homesteads were being attacked regularly by groups of armed assailants.)

A few days later, I again made my way to Peter's farm. Peter was a strong believer in God and had experienced active angelic protection from armed assailants on at least two occasions. I had agreed to "brightlight" over the weekend and planned to return early to school on Monday morning, a trip of about forty kilometers (twenty-four miles). Peter's farmhouse stood on an acre lot on elevated terrain, making it ideal for 360-degree surveillance. On subsequent visits, Peter and I would rise early and spend time together in Bible reading and prayer in the "upper room," a tower-like structure adjoining the west side of the house. The golden sunrise over the African bush and sparkling reflections on the nearby dam were awe-inspiring.

The farmstead was surrounded by an eight-foot-high security fence with barbed wire overhang strung along the top, designed to keep armed attackers at bay. Homemade "grenade launchers" were mounted on each of the four corners. In the center of the farmhouse, adjacent to a large living room and juxtaposed between a hallway and spacious kitchen, was a sandbag "fort-like" bunker structure measuring about four feet by three feet at the base and six feet high supported with four large upright wooden poles. This was the "central command" last stand center where emergency communications could be made to neighboring farmers. It was also stocked with extra weapons and emergency food and water. From this homemade "command center," one could gauge the direction of guerrilla-terrorist fire and activate the homemade grenade launchers, which were filled with nails and bolts. The shrapnel from the explosions was potentially deadly.

The weekend was uneventful—no guerrilla-terrorist attacks. I was on the road at sunrise Monday morning and on my way to teach my amazing "standard four" (fifth-grade) kiddos. I loved my students. I was conscious of the time and pressed the accelerator. The steep dirt road was strewn with quartz-like rocks and was slippery at best. To my right was the wooded hillside. A grader had moved rocks and dirt into three-foot high oblique ridges to direct floodwaters along the side of the road. However, there was no rain on this winter's day. To my left was a tree-covered escarpment. There was no safety rail to stop one from careening down the hillside to certain death.

I crested the hill and was momentarily blinded by the blazing sunlight. A large rock, the size of a soccer ball, was in the center of this narrow bush road. I swerved instinctively to my right and skated toward the hillside and rock-dirt mounds. I immediately spun the steering wheel to the left while still skating toward the hill. At the very last second, the vehicle veered to the left. I was gaining momentum down a long, slippery, rocky dirt road and was sliding uncontrollably toward the hill's precipice. Instinctively, as though an angel was guiding my hands, I spun the steering wheel to the right to correct my overcorrection. I should have disappeared down the escarpment to certain death or plowed into the mountainside and been killed, but somehow my vehicle snaked its way down about two-thirds of the steep decline, momentum building until BOOM!

My Datsun was catapulted through the air and landed with a jolt on a hillside ridge. All was quiet. Deathly quiet.

I pinched myself to see if I was still alive. Ouch! Then slowly I checked my body over. No apparent breaks. I scrambled out of the vehicle to inspect the damage. The white Datsun was suspended over the hillside ridge. The front left wheel had been crushed, but amazingly the tire was still inflated. The left rear wheel was suspended. I checked the back of the vehicle. There was hardly a scratch. How could this be? I tried starting my car, but the "grounded" right rear wheel dug deeper and deeper into the dirt mound. I slung my LPD semi-automatic over my shoulder and looked both ways. I was about twelve miles from Peter's farm and another eighteen miles from school. I decided to walk back toward the farm.

In my haste to get to school early, I had not had my normal "quiet time" devotional prayer and Bible time with the Lord. I opened my small Gideon's New Testament. My eyes fell on Matthew 7, verses 7 and 8: *"Ask and it will be given to you; seek and you will find; knock and the door will be opened to you. For everyone who asks receives; the one who seeks finds; and to the one who knocks, the door will be opened"* (NIV). God's Word burned in my heart. I began to weep. How timely the Word of God was in my time of need. I prayed earnestly with hot tears flowing. "Father, You know where I am at. You have saved my life today. You know that I need to be back to teach my students. Father, please send a miracle. Thank You for sending a miracle."

I continued walking slowly up the steep incline. Minutes went by that seemed more like hours. The stillness of the early African morning was invigorating. God was in this place. I was at peace. There was no possibility of escaping this situation and certainly no possibility of arriving at school on time to teach my students. And then, almost imperceptibly at first, the sound of a tractor permeated the still morning air. My mind immediately dismissed the possibility of the tractor coming this way. It was probably native workers crossing the road from one farm to another. Why the doubt, though? My ears perked as the sound appeared to be coming closer. A few minutes later, a tractor pulling a trailer full of African farm workers mounted the horizon and chugged steadily down the hill.

The driver stopped the diesel tractor but kept it running. The starter apparently did not work, so he had to keep it idling. He asked what had happened. I told him the story and pointed out the skid marks made by my careening car down the mountainside. "Ah, boss, you should be dead. There is no way you can be alive. No way," the driver exclaimed. The workers chimed in similarly. I then told them about Jesus and how He'd saved my life as I careened out of control down the mountain. "Sure, God has saved you. Sure! Sure!" they exclaimed.

The workers gathered around my car and heaved it up and over the dirt. The left front tire rim looked like an orange that had the top third removed. I was awestruck at how the vehicle had not been demolished. I thanked the workers, who were like God's angels to me, and started back to school. My confidence grew as the road leveled. Soon I was on a tarred road heading back to my hometown and school. I squeezed the accelerator to 120 km/h. The students had their teacher that morning—and just on time, too. Little did they know what my early morning activities had been. God had heard my humble cry for help, and He answered. "*The god who answers by fire—he is God*" (1 Kings 18:24b, NIV).

God had protected me from the firestorms and spared my life. He had helped me *soar above the storms*. But then I felt a shift in wind patterns and another sudden temperature change....

Shirley's Reflections

Living in the city, I didn't see much guerrilla-terrorist action. Most men had to do military training (up to age forty). Those who had already trained had to do their part. The men would serve for six weeks, then have six weeks off, continuously. My brother-in-law had injured his back as his military vehicle hit a landmine. This affected the workplace and home life. It disrupted life in every area. Many young men in my church were killed, and when I was in the workforce, many of my coworkers lost their husbands. There was always a funeral to attend. A sad time indeed.

CHAPTER 3

Fully Immersed

(1979-1980)

Crisis Faced: Obedience to God's Word
Crisis: Spiritual – To Be Like Jesus
Storm: Monsoon – Heavy Rains

Spiritual Growth

I regularly attended the Catholic church early in my first year of teaching at Shabani Primary in Zvishavane, Zimbabwe. Then my female teacher friend Joey invited me to the local Assembly of God with the promise of lively music and lovely people. I attended and thoroughly enjoyed the services, music and down-to-earth people. Then one day a new mining friend sat on his motorcycle outside my front door and challenged me to examine where I was being fed spiritually. I was still Catholic to the core and attended the Catholic church mainly out of duty and tradition. I pondered his question and did some soul-searching. God wasn't Catholic or Pentecostal. There are no church denominations in heaven, only people who love Jesus. I slowly transitioned to the Assembly of God church. Dennis, a single father who loved Jesus passionately and played the accordion, regularly invited Ann and Joey, two other first-year teachers, and me to Sunday lunch. These were festive occasions with great food, conversations about Jesus and the Bible, and music. I loved Sundays.

The resident Assembly of God pastor and his wife were called to a different church, but we still held lively congregation-led services. One Sunday evening we had a guest speaker named Neil Rhodes. Neil was a young pastor passing through Shabani on his way to South Africa. He was visiting his in-laws in Shabani. Neil had been radically saved from a life of rebellion and drugs several years prior and immediately entered Bible school. A few years later, he became the principal of the Bible school. Neil preached a fiery and impacting message about an eagle and how it soars on thermals and has keen "double vision." It could look upwards and peer earthwards. Neil drew the analogy of us "rising on the wings of eagles" and "looking toward heaven" while not neglecting our earthly responsibilities. The key scripture verse was Isaiah 40:31: *"But they that wait upon the Lord shall renew their strength; they shall mount up with wings as eagles; they shall run, and not be weary; and they shall walk, and not faint"* (KJV). I never forgot this message.

Neil was offered a position at the local non-denominational church a few miles away near the elementary school. I was hungry for the Word of God and eager to grow spiritually. I decided to visit the non-denominational church. Ann came, too. Neil's sermons were challenging and meaty and preached with fiery passion as though God was pleading for "sinners" to make themselves right with Him and receive eternal life. There was also plenty of faith teaching. *"For we walk by faith, not by sight"* (2 Corinthians 5:7, KJV).

Neil held Bible studies at his home where he taught us the Bible in depth. I couldn't get enough. He then started holding in-home Bible studies for church families in distant bush communities such as Belingwe (now Mberengwa) and the mining village at Buckwa. Neil drove on dirt roads like the devil himself was chasing him. The palms of my hands would sweat profusely when I rode with him. Sometimes, just Ann and I would travel and lead the Bible studies.

Baptisms

One night, I attended a local house fellowship meeting led by Desmond and his wife, Sheila. Desmond worked for the local town council and had earlier conscripted me as the Presiding Officer to oversee national elections way out in the bush. We were discussing Matthew chapter 3.

Verses 13 through 17 struck me, especially verse 15: "*Then Jesus came from Galilee to the Jordan to be baptized by John. But John tried to deter him, saying, 'I need to be baptized by you, and do you come to me?' Jesus replied, 'Let it be so now; it is proper for us to do this to fulfill all righteousness.' Then John consented. As soon as Jesus was baptized, he went up out of the water. At that moment heaven was opened, and he saw the Spirit of God descending like a dove and alighting on him. And a voice from heaven said, 'This is my Son, whom I love; with him I am well pleased'*" (NIV, emphasis added).

I wanted to be like Jesus. I could see Him living in many Christians I knew, especially Neil and his wife, Noline. Neil would give his monthly salary away and "live by faith," trusting God to meet his needs. Without fail, God always met his needs. This total abandonment to the purposes of God was deeply impacting. Furthermore, Neil had asked me to prepare a message on "baptisms" to share in the outreach Bible meetings. I had no idea what he was talking about. The only baptism I knew of was sprinkling as an infant. But then Neil taught us the meaning of the Greek word for "baptism," *baptizo*, which means to be fully immersed in water. When I explained my conundrum to Neil, he offered me a book titled *They Speak with Other Tongues* by John Sherrill. I consumed the book. And now Desmond was sharing on Jesus' baptism. The thought struck me that if Jesus had to be baptized to "*fulfill all righteousness*," then I also needed to be baptized, just like Jesus. Verse 16 also grabbed my attention: "*As soon as Jesus was baptized, he went up out of the water. At that moment heaven was opened, and he saw the Spirit of God descending like a dove and alighting on him.*" Jesus came "*up out of the water*," implying that He had been "down in the water"—fully immersed—and then the Holy Spirit descended on Jesus. Acts 2:38 says, "*And Peter said to them, 'Repent and be baptized every one of you in the name of Jesus Christ for the forgiveness of your sins, and you will receive the gift of the Holy Spirit'*" (ESV).

The following Sunday was baptism Sunday. A crude concrete block baptismal had been built outdoors at the back of the country church. One other lady and I were slated for water baptism. I could hardly wait. In fact, I was so focused on being baptized after the evening service that I had not thought about a towel or change of clothing. I was dressed in my gray suit and tie. A single exterior light shone near the baptismal. The lady was baptized first. Then it was my turn. I quickly removed my suit jacket and shirt tie and mounted the block steps. Neil was waiting. "I baptize you in the name of the Father, and the Son, and…the Holy Spirit." I was plunged forward beneath the crystal-clear cool water. Fully immersed, just like Jesus. When I surfaced, Neil laid his hands on my head and prayed for the baptism of the Holy Spirit. What bold faith. What gentleness. With gentle encouragement, I opened my mouth and began speaking utterances in a language I had never learned, haltingly at first, but soon in a flowing language—a heavenly language. The Holy Spirit had come on Jesus, and He had come on me, too. Oh, the beauty of His majesty. How powerful the name of Jesus. He is truly no respecter of people.

God's Voice

I drove home slowly to the men's mess. The streets were mostly quite well-lit with tall neon fluorescent streetlamps. I unlocked the front door and walked over to the dining room table. I sat down and picked up a blue airmail letter—the kind we used to send overseas. The previous night I had had a dream about Shirley, whom I'd dated a few years before when I attended the Hillside Teachers' College in Bulawayo. I had been praying fervently for God's choice of marriage partner for several months. I had even dated a nurse in training from Salisbury (now Harare). The relationship with the nurse was mainly by letter, but then the letters stopped. No explanation was ever given. I learned that God always answers prayers. The answer is either yes, no or maybe. This answer was a resolute no. No! And then Shirley popped up in my dreams.

Shirley had emigrated to England but remembered me on my birthday, Easter and Christmas. In one of my replies, I told Shirley that God had someone very special for her. It was my way of trying to redirect Shirley's outreach efforts as I had resolved to move on from the relationship. I had even torn up her letters. However, I could not tear up her picture, which I kept in my wallet. And then I had that dream. It was as though God was saying, "You've prayed. I've answered. Here is My choice of a bride for your life."

Little did I know that Shirley was in England on her face before God, pleading, "Take these feelings away that I have for Martin or do something to him." I have always believed James 5:16, which in its talk about healing says this: "*The effectual fervent prayer of a righteous man availeth much*" (KJV). Later I realized that for Shirley, her prayers availed *very* much. And God answered my prayers, too.

As I sat at the dining room table filled to overflowing with the newly received gift of the Holy Spirit baptism, I heard the voice of God. Loudly. Internally. "*Write to Shirley and ask her to marry you.*" I sat dumbfounded. Transfixed. God's voice had exploded inside my spirit. I knew it was God. Then my fleshly analytical mind kicked in. How could I just write a letter to someone I hadn't seen in years? She may even be married. Then it was as though the Holy Spirit allowed me to see ten years down the road. I would still be praying for God's perfect will regarding a partner for my life—and would have missed it so badly. I picked up the blue ballpoint pen and began writing.

"Dear Shirley, how would you consider an extended relationship…?" The letter continued a page or more. I did not use the word *marriage* for fear of rejection, even though God had explicitly told me what to write….

I mailed the letter first thing the next morning and felt I had been obedient to God. When Shirley received the letter, she fasted and prayed for three days and then replied. I received her reply three weeks later. It went something like this: "Dear Martin, if you feel this is the Lord's leading, then come over to England, and let's see what God has for us. I have Christian friends you can stay with… Love, Shirley."

Rhema Word

It was a Friday. I froze when I received Shirley's letter. God was serious. I immediately started three days of prayer and fasting. Amazingly, my northern Irish non-churchgoing Protestant mother called me later that day and strongly urged me to "come and see the real thing." She then described what sounded like a move of the Spirit that had everyone prostrate on the ground. Apparently a German evangelist by the name of Reinhard Bonnke had set up a massive tent in the Mucheke Township a few miles from my parents' home. "You've got to come and see this," my mother urged.

I drove to my parents' home on Saturday and attended the tent service. The tent was overflowing with over 10,000 people, mainly local

Africans, in attendance. I had never experienced the electrifying, powerful presence of the Holy Spirit. I recall singing one verse of one praise chorus for over an hour. Heaven came down to earth that night. People were saved, healed and delivered from witchcraft. Droves of locals ran forward to the front of the tent and pitched their witchcraft paraphernalia into a heap. God was at work doing only what He could do. I was forever changed and remember whispering to God, "If You call me, I will serve You and do whatever You say."

I drove back to Shabani the following day, Sunday. In my devotions for the day, one Bible verse spoke to me. I had been asking God for a confirming word as Neil always taught us. I had to have a Scripture to stand on in times of trial and doubt. God spoke plainly to my spirit in the context of marriage through 1 Chronicles 28:20: "*David also said to Solomon his son, 'Be strong and courageous, **and do the work**. Do not be afraid or discouraged, for the Lord God, my God, is with you. He will not fail you or forsake you until all the work for the service of the temple of the Lord is finished*'" (NIV, emphasis added). In the context of seeking God's will in marriage, the Holy Spirit strongly impressed on my heart that I was to be strong and courageous and that He was doing the work. He would not fail or forsake me. I understood that the text was originally talking about building the temple, but God made it plain to me that the "temple" in this rhema word was marriage.

I had "survived" the deluge of a spiritual monsoon and risen *above the storms*. Little did I realize that monsoons can spawn other storms....

Shirley's Reflections

I was so excited when I received Martin's letter, although it was not a marriage proposal. I wanted to know that he was serious, so I told him he had to come to England. I was not returning to Africa unless I knew his intent. I even went and picked out a ring.

CHAPTER 4
Airborne
(1980-1981)

Crisis Faced: Marriage – Male and Female
Crisis: Faith – Dead Without Works
Storm: Tornado – Violently Rotating Winds

Steps of Faith

Once God confirmed in my heart His direction concerning a wife, I shared with my pastor, Neil, and close friends in the church who resonated with what God was doing. I was a teacher on a lean income. I did not have significant savings. I cashed in the life insurance my father had taken out for me, fully believing that God would take care of me. I remember when the agent (a friend of my father's) came to my home and tried to dissuade me from making "a foolish mistake." I told him confidently that "God was taking care of me." As I said those words, an African mask set on a ledge above the living room curtains and leaning backward on the wall suddenly capitulated and tumbled forward, smashing into pieces on the hard red stone floor. Apparently the demons could not handle the newfound confidence in God and scrambled—literally—and so did the insurance agent. I had not knowingly invited demons into my home, but nevertheless, they were there. Not anymore!

I went to the sole travel agency in Shabani and booked an airline ticket from Bulawayo, Zimbabwe, to London, England. The flight was full, but I was placed on the reserve list. I responded to Shirley's letter and asked if she would be able to meet me in London. She wasn't. I spoke to the local Barclay's bank manager, a Christian in our church, who was aware of my situation and painlessly forwarded the amount I needed to cover the ticket. The insurance rebate of $150 covered my spending money for England.

Ray, a college buddy of mine, had become radically saved at college. One day he was standing on a chair in the student recreation center championing his freedoms as a liberal thinker; the next day he responded to an invitation to follow Christ at an outreach service. He repented of his sins, took up his "cross," and began sharing Jesus with all who would listen.

Ray invited me to join his friend and renowned Oxford-educated youth leader, Chris Hingley, at a youth camp at the beginning of the Christmas school holiday. My overseas flight was toward the end of the camp, so I contacted Shirley's parents who lived in Bulawayo and asked if I could leave my vehicle with them and if they would drop me at the airport. I also asked if I could spend a night with them on my way to the youth camp. They agreed. They also agreed to pick me up at the airport upon my return a week later. Shirley's parents were excited when I told them why I was going to England, and Shirley's mother gave me a letter to give to Shirley upon my arrival. I later found out that Shirley's mother was "keeping her fingers crossed." In retrospect, I never asked directly for Shirley's parents' blessing. I was so focused on "obeying God and going to England" that it completely slipped my mind. For that, I am very sorry. *Sorry, Mom and Dad Sallabank.* Thankfully, they gave their blessing without my asking.

Tuli River

The youth camp was in the southwestern part of the country, several hours away in total isolation in a place called the Tuli Circle on the banks of the Tuli River. Once off the main tarred road, the dirt road was bone-shaking, and I wondered if my white Datsun would make it. It did. Just ninety years prior, pioneers had ventured from South Africa and set up camp in the Tuli Circle. They even built a small hotel. The pieces of evidence of the first pioneers lay scattered throughout the bush. They had crossed the Tuli River with their ox-drawn covered wagons and continued into the interior of virgin territory, which was later named Rhodesia after Cecil John Rhodes.

I joined the Baptist youth group on the banks of the Tuli River. They had arrived the previous day and already set up camp. My "camp" was a sleeping bag under the stars. Hopefully the bright blazing fire would keep lions and leopards at bay. I remember lying there looking up at the brilliant diamond-sparkling stars when Ray asked me, "So, Marty, tell me again why you are going to England." I told him my story. Again. He just could not believe it. "God told you to marry Shirley, so you're going to England to ask her to marry you?" he quizzed incredulously. I was still becoming familiar with all the Bible stories and had not thought to give him examples of "arranged" marriages such as Isaac and Rebekah or Boaz and Ruth.

The week was filled with hiking and exploring adventures, which included fording the flooded Tuli River. The week sped by, and it was soon time for me to drive back to Bulawayo. I was low on gas and out of money since I put everything toward going to see Shirley. Amazingly, I made it over the rugged corrugated dirt roads and onto the main paved road back to Shirley's hometown of Bulawayo. God supplied my needs by prompting someone at a gas station to put ten dollars' worth of gas in my vehicle. This was enough to make it to Bulawayo. God answers prayer! *"And my God shall supply all your need according to His riches in glory by Christ Jesus"* (Philippians 4:19, NKJV).

Proposal

I arrived at Shirley's parents' home in Bulawayo with just one hour to get ready to leave for the airport. I had a bath and readied myself for the trip. My bags had already been packed. Shirley's parents drove me to the airport and waved goodbye. They had known me from several years back when I was at the Teachers' College (TTC). I had played ping-pong with Shirley's dad, who was an avid and accomplished player. I also enjoyed the weekly Saturday salad lunches that Shirley's mom made. Incredulously, I even ate cow's tongue and enjoyed it. This was uncharacteristic

31

of me, as I tend to "imagine" the animal or part thereof being consumed. Fortunately, I had no knowledge of the type of meat it was at the time. We said our goodbyes at the airport. Soon I was winging my way to the capital city of Salisbury (now Harare) where I would catch an overnight flight to London.

The flight was uneventful. I caught a bus from London to the town of Rugby, about a three-hour trip. I was amazed at the driver's skill in navigating narrow roads so deftly.

Shirley had lived in Rugby for two years. She had felt God's clear leading to leave her homeland of Zimbabwe and move to England. Her British parents, Miles and Edna Sallabank, followed suit a few months later based on a job offer Mr. Sallabank had had on a previous visit. However, the economy had gone belly-up when he arrived in the UK, and the job offers had evaporated. The Sallabanks turned their shipping crates around at port and sent them back to Zimbabwe. Fortunately, Mr. Sallabank was reinstated in his job on the railways, but they had lost their prized possession, an upscale home with a high ornate stone wall surrounding the property. They settled for a lesser home and were thankful to be back.

Excitement tickled inside as the coach neared Rugby. Shirley had explained in a letter that she was not able to meet me in London but would meet me at the bus depot in Rugby. I spotted her immediately among a small crowd. Her face was beaming despite the winter chill and snow on the ground. My heart leaped. I greeted Shirley warmly and was introduced to some of her friends. I had come to England for one month over the Zimbabwe Christmas school holidays. Shirley was slated to work until Christmas and had taken leave from work for the remainder of my stay.

I stayed with Tony and Nancy, a lovely middle-aged couple who had three teen children. They were leaders in the local Baptist church and godly people. Shirley boarded with the most wonderful Jehovah's Witness couple who treated her with kindness and respect. They also provided meals for Shirley. I was included in these meals on several occasions. One evening shortly after my arrival, Shirley and I were eating a meal at Shirley's host's home. We were alone looking at pictures of Shirley's friends, including a former "boyfriend" from the Teachers' College whom I knew. He was a nice chap but shorter than Shirley.

"You didn't date him, surely not?" I joshed. *Jealousy 101!* We laughed. The topic soon turned to *our* relationship. I felt a stirring in my spirit and was uncharacteristically nervous.

"So, will you?" I asked, alluding to marriage.

"Will I what?" Shirley quizzed knowingly.

"You know. Will you?" I repeated giggling. I normally giggle when I am nervous.

"Will I what?" Shirley asked questioningly, at first with eyes wide open, then leaning forward slightly, eyes narrowing. It was clear that Shirley wanted me to say exactly what was on my mind and not to keep her guessing. It was also clear that she "knew" intuitively what I was trying to articulate without actually saying it. But she would have none of it.

"Will you…marry me?" I blurted, my face flushing.

I had not rehearsed this moment. I was simply "going with the flow" of God's Spirit and found myself asking Shirley to marry me.

"Yes, I will marry you," Shirley replied pensively.

"You will?" I gasped. "Really?"

Engagement

We became engaged nine days after I arrived in Rugby, England, on New Year's Eve, December 31, 1980.

Shirley had already visited a jeweler before my arrival and knew exactly what ring she wanted. A ruby ring. I foolishly insisted that Shirley have a diamond ring based on the false and popular notion that "diamonds are a woman's best friend." Shirley yielded but always regretted not having the ruby ring. I attempted to correct this error forty years later when I bought Shirley a blood-red ruby ring. She was delighted. "*A wife of noble character who can find? She is worth far more than rubies*" (Proverbs 31:10, NIV). The Lord impressed Esther 8:8 on my spirit at this time. The inscription is on our wedding rings. "*Now write another decree in the king's name in behalf of the Jews as seems best to you, and seal it with the king's signet ring—for no document written in the king's name and **sealed with his ring** can be revoked*" (NIV, emphasis added). I was convinced that God was serious about marriage being a lifetime covenant—"until death do us part."

My money was spent mostly on Shirley's engagement and wedding rings. Shirley graciously used her meager savings to purchase tickets across to Ireland for us to meet some of my rarely visited relatives. We had memorable and fun times on the coaches, trains and ferry and learned some "Kerryman" riddle jokes, which we used as teasers with friends for years. We also met Shirley's relatives in England. One relative was Shirley's Aunt Muriel, or "Murweal," as some British may say.

Since it was the Christmas season, Aunt "Murweal" served up some British mince pies. These are small pastry tarts filled with "raisin mince" and covered with a small pastry lid. My eyes caught a mince pie with its lid partly lifted, showing the inside dark mince. I started laughing uncontrollably. I had never done this before. The more I laughed, the louder I got. Soon I was rolling on the carpet in raucous laughter. Shirley had no idea what was going on and was a bit bewildered at first. However, soon she, too, was in full-swing laughter mode. And before long, Aunt "Murweal" let down her guard and joined in the fun.

The trigger for the laughter had come from an event six months prior. I was returning from a road trip to South Africa with my college teacher friend Marianne. Marianne and I had been in the same year at Teachers' College. We had served at a youth camp together at Victoria Falls under the leadership of my friends Chris Hingley and Ray Pountney. Ray had the bright idea that Marianne and I should travel together since we both wanted to visit friends in South Africa. This seemed to make sense since there was still an element of danger at the winding down of the Bush War.

On our way back from South Africa, about an hour north of the Beitbridge, a small border post on the southernmost part of Zimbabwe, we came across an accident. The road was totally deserted. A crunched-up vehicle was on the side of the road. My car beams cut through the charcoal night sky. I pulled over on my side of the road and told Mariane to stay put. I was a British Red Cross-trained "first aid" instructor and had experience dealing with a variety of injuries. However, no amount of training could have prepared me for what I was about to witness.

Fatal Accident
According to one African semitruck driver, the driver of the vehicle, a four-door sedan, had plowed into the back of the semi at high speed

just two minutes prior. The other semi driver had gone to Beitbridge to notify the police for assistance. There were three African passengers in the vehicle—two in the front and one in the back. I used a flashlight and switched to emergency take-charge "first aid" mode. The occupants were still and warm to touch. None of the occupants had worn a seatbelt. This was common since most cars were not equipped with seatbelts. I tried checking the driver's wrist for a pulse, but his arm was bent like a twig and hanging on by a "bacon" strip of skin. No pulse in his other wrist. One deceased. I tried the passenger in the back. No pulse. Broken neck from hitting the car ceiling. Deceased number two. The lady in the front passenger seat was a heavily endowed and outsized person. Her chin was perched on the dashboard and her large body was thrust under the dashboard. Rolls of flesh joined her neck to her head. Since I could not reach her wrist to take her pulse, I tried her neck. However, the fleshly rolls impeded my attempts to locate her pulse. I instinctively grabbed the tufts of hair on her forehead and lifted her head in an attempt to tilt it backward. Her head remained put but her "lid" lifted. The impact of the vehicle had cracked the top of the skull open much like one might crack an egg when frying it. I peered into "grey" matter. Three deceased. All warm. All still.

This scene flashed through my mind when I saw the mince pie with its lid cracked open at "Aunt Murweal's." The PTSD "shock" had finally caught up with me and was being processed through laughter. Indeed, there was nothing inherently "funny" about this situation, but the thirty-five minutes of uncontrolled belly-aching, gully-washer laughter brought great release and inner healing to the terrible trauma. God's Word was true again. "*A cheerful heart is good medicine, but a crushed spirit dries up the bones*" (Proverbs 17:22, NIV).

Wedding Plans

Our days together in England and Ireland were spent in jovial laughter and fellowship. We both loved Jesus and dreamed about our future together. Soon it was mid-January 1981 and time for me to return to Zimbabwe and my elementary school in Zvishavane for the start of a new school year. Shirley gave notice at her banking job, canceled the upcoming closing on a flat (apartment), and made travel arrangements to Zimbabwe, leaving in mid-March. Once there, she stayed with her parents about five hours away by car and made a couple of weekend visits over the next several weeks. She stayed at the "girls' mess" (lady teachers' house about a mile away). We planned our wedding together, but Shirley handled most of the church and flower arrangements as we planned to be married in her home city and former church, the Bulawayo Baptist Church, on April 25, 1981. We could see no sense in delaying the wedding.

One weekend when Shirley visited, we attended the local Assembly of God church where Neil had been a guest speaker. They still did not have a full-time pastor but were actively seeking a replacement. Neil had arranged for a missionary pastor to Zimbabwe from America to be the guest speaker. Pastor David Garcia preached an alliteration sermon where each point began with the letter "d." "What happens when you depart from God? Decision…deception…depression… despair…." He preached a powerful message by the power of the Holy Spirit. He also had a "word of knowledge" that was convicting. I knew God was speaking to me.

Fast forward many years—I met Pastor David Garcia in Brooksville, Florida, USA, in April of 1997. I was being considered as the new school administrator at a local Christian school where Pastor Garcia's wife, Nellie, was teaching Spanish. "Sister" Nellie called Pastor Garcia and told him that she had met a man they knew from Africa. Pastor Garcia immediately drove to the school and burst into the office where I was in the middle of an interview. Everyone knew Pastor and Nellie Garcia. "Didn't you have a beard in Zimbabwe?" he asked excitedly. We talked for a while. The interview committee was excited. I think this unplanned "intrusion" did not hinder the interview outcome as I was later offered the position.

Shirley and I continued to plan and pray for our wedding by phone, mainly. We were excited, as were Shirley's parents. However, my dad had difficulty receiving the news of our choice of church. He expected me to be married in a Catholic church after the way I had been raised. I explained over the phone a situation where someone was booked into a fancy hotel (Catholic church) where the food was okay but not great. Down the street was a little café (non-denominational charismatic church) with mouthwatering food. I then said, "Where would you eat, Dad?" He immediately concurred that he would eat at the café. This little illustration helped ease his acceptance of my marrying a "Protestant" in a "Protestant" church. However, a few days later, I received a phone call from my mother. She explained that Dad had spoken to the local Catholic priest about the situation. The priest told him in no uncertain terms that he was not to attend the wedding since a Catholic priest was not officiating. He also said that my dad would be denied the sacraments if he attended. This was like cutting the heart and soul out of a Catholic. I knew. I had been raised Catholic. Also, he was mandated to inform each family member to cancel attendance. I could tell my mother was shaken and not in agreement. However, she stood by my father.

Shirley was devastated when I told her the news. The wedding was just days away, and she had changed plans to accommodate the absence of my father—and now my whole family couldn't come. She would have to change the corsage plans again. Shirley and I prayed about what this would mean. We certainly did not want my side of the family to be absent. We envisioned them not being there and the long-term impact this would have on our marriage and our relationship with my parents. I loved my parents. Shirley cared for them, too, but she could not understand the vice-like grip the Catholic religion had on my father. I understood. He loved me dearly as a son but felt trapped. He could not deny his religion to appease his son.

A few days later, my mother called a charismatic Catholic priest who happened to be in the area. She explained the situation and invited him to the house. The priest explained to my dad that *"love covers over a multitude of sins,"* and that it would be okay for him to attend our wedding. I received another phone call from my mother. Good news! Shirley again changed the corsage arrangements. My family would be there after all. *Thank You, Jesus!* *"Above all, love each other deeply, because love covers over a multitude of sins"* (1 Peter 4:8, NIV).

Church Camp

We had a church camp one weekend, but Shirley could not find a ride and was unable to come. Our church camped out on the shores of Lake Kyle (now Lake Mutirikwe) about ninety miles from my town. Canadian traveling evangelist Hugh Crookshank was asked to be a guest speaker at this camp. Neil was on his annual itinerary. Pastor Hugh was from a Pentecostal church in Canada and relied heavily on the Holy Spirit for everything. He told the story of how one day he was at an international airport. He was obedient to the Holy Spirit but did not have the funds needed. Suddenly, an individual in the line walked up to him and said he felt impressed by God to bless him financially. It was exactly what Pastor Hugh needed for his ticket. He had many other stories of God's miraculous provision.

We arrived on a Friday afternoon. Hugh preached a simple but faith-building message that evening that concluded in prayer. I was kneeling in prayer and crying out to God for His presence. I also believed in Him for taking care of our upcoming wedding and for my left ear to be healed from deafness. The presence of God touched me tangibly. A numbness started in my lips, then flushed up my forehead and down my arms and entire body. It was as though I was completely "frozen" in the tangible presence of Almighty God. I was unable to move, and neither did I want to. "Oh, the glory of His presence…." I basked in the glory of God's tangible presence for about an hour and slowly, with assistance, made my way to my cabin. God's tangible manifestation of tingly numbness remained with me most of the night. The peace and power of the Holy Spirit completely overhauled my biological senses. And God answered my wedding prayers.

Married

Shirley and I had been praying about the wedding and for wisdom in responding to my parents' (my father's) insistence on at least having a Catholic priest perform the wedding ceremony. After this weekend, I felt the Lord pointing me to Psalm 7:15: *"He made a pit, and digged it, and is fallen into the ditch which he made"* (KJV). It was as though the veil was lifted from my eyes, and I could see clearly. My dad had fallen into a religious pit and was unable to dig himself out. Thankfully, God had other plans.

We were married in Shirley's home church, the Bulawayo Baptist Church, on April 25, 1981. Neil (our Shabani pastor) performed the marriage ceremony. David Stevenson, a friend and local District

Commissioner at Belingwe (Mberengwa), near Shabani (Zvishavane), transferred his jurisdiction to Bulawayo for a day so that he could perform the legal side of the wedding. Peter (my farmer friend) was my best man, and my two younger brothers, Brian and Liam, were groomsmen. Shirley's eldest sister, Jane, was the maid of honor. Liz, Shirley's best friend, and my sister, Mary, were bridesmaids. Shirley's youngest sister, Lee, was a flower girl.

The wedding party was staged. I peered longingly down the aisle with breathless anticipation for the entrance of my beautiful bride-to-be. I did not have long to wait. The organ ripped through the silence and announced Shirley's arrival. Soon Shirley's silhouette filled the back doorway, tall and slim, with a long flowing dress and a veil covering her eyes. Her arm was linked to her father's, Miles Sallabank. Shirley glided gracefully down the aisle. The soft white neon lights cascaded over her beautiful form. My heart skipped a beat or two. This was the one the Lord had chosen for me. How perfect was His gift. How awesome is our God! I was reminded of James 1:17, "*Every good gift and every perfect gift is from above, and comes down from the Father of lights, with whom there is no variation or shadow of turning*" (NKJV). When Shirley was about a third of the way down the aisle, I could see her face through the veil. Shirley was effervescent, her smile radiating in beams of incandescent light pulsating through the church. I noticed her eyes fluttering like the soft white wings of a butterfly flitting from flower to flower. She was deliriously rapturous, my beloved Shirley—"lily of the valley."

Soon the ceremony was underway. We sang two hymns: "Blessed Assurance," previously selected by Shirley, and "How Great Thou Art," selected by me. I noticed my dad wiping his eyes. I later discovered that they sang this same song at the Catholic church a week later. Dad was deeply touched. Shirley's mom sang a wedding blessing that she wrote to the tune of the hymn, "Search Me, O God," by James E. Orr (1936). One line I recall went like this: "Bless Thee, O Lord, this marriage here today." We pledged our lives to God and each other and entered the covenant of marriage with God at the center. We exchanged rings. Our gold rings had Esther 8:8 inscribed on the inside. God had spoken.

We had wedding pictures taken at the lush green Bulawayo Centenary Park among the kaleidoscope of gladioli flowers. It was a picture-perfect

African fall day (like October can be in parts of America). The reception was held in the Baptist church hall. My sister Mary and younger brother Liam sang "Come to the Waters." Mary played the guitar. My mother gave a toast and awarded Shirley a trophy for the "world's best long-distance angler." Apparently she thought Shirley had been fishing for me. Little did she know that God had arranged our steps. In retrospect, I think Mom had privileged insight. God had answered Shirley's deepest, heartfelt prayer five thousand miles away when she was in England: "Do something to Martin or take these feelings from me." God *did* something to me. George Jenkinson, Sr. (whom I'd never met), was the emcee. Shirley knew him and had chosen well.

By late afternoon, Mr. and Mrs. Ratcliffe, newlyweds, were loaded up in the shiny white Datsun and on the road to Beitbridge, a border town on the southern Zimbabwean border several hours away.

Honeymoon

The trip was uneventful. The night was black. The stars shone brilliantly like the little diamonds on Shirley's wedding ring. The road was bereft of traffic. We played gospel tapes and talked most of the way to the border. About ten miles out, there was a hitchhiker. I stopped and backed up. The hitchhiker needed to get to the border before it closed. I dropped Shirley at the Beitbridge Hotel and promised a soon return. Bad move. I was trying to help a fellow earth citizen stranded in the middle of nowhere, but this was our wedding night. Perhaps I could have dropped him at the hotel where he could have summoned a taxi to the border. I didn't. I had still to learn that my wife was my number one ministry.

We departed midmorning the next day for South Africa. Across the wide Limpopo River lay South Africa and our destination, the small holiday town of Tshipese, about seventy-five miles from Zimbabwe's southern border. I had reserved a place for us to honeymoon with the knowledgeable assistance of Neil, our pastor. (Actually, Neil booked it, and I paid him back.) We honeymooned for about ten days. Tshipese was renowned for its hot sulfur springs. The resort was all-inclusive and had tennis courts and a pool.

Shirley and I had previously played squash when I was at the Bulawayo Hillside Teachers' College and dating her. She was a good squash player, but I did not count on those skills transferring to tennis. My tennis ego was quickly deflated as Shirley beat me quite soundly in the first few games. She wasn't kidding when she said she played on Eveline High School's first (varsity) tennis team. Humble pie for me. (Her tennis prowess continues to this day, but in the form of pickleball, which requires less running. Her cross-court shots continue to amaze me.) The surprised look on my face and demeanor must have been noticeable and had Shirley in stitches. She was enjoying this immensely, relishing every moment. I composed myself just as Shirley was tiring. Fortunately, this was to my advantage, and I rebounded to win the set. Whew!

Over the years, Shirley has delighted in beating me in table tennis and in anything competitive, including Scrabble. She says that she does not have this competitive desire against others. "O, Lord, it's hard to be humble," the country song goes—but not so hard when my wife beats me in some sport or game. We also play "last touch" and have had some seriously hilarious moments when neither of us will give in. This "game" (passed on by our mothers) seems to have trickled its way down to our children and grandchildren with much hilarity.

For much of the honeymoon, I was unusually tired. I was often very tired at the end of a very active school term and spent the first couple of weeks of the school vacation recovering. This left me with another two weeks to get ready for the next term. We were in the first two weeks, but the tiredness was unusual even with the normal school fatigue. I found out later that I had had bilharzia, a parasitic water-borne disease prevalent throughout Africa and other parts of the world. I had probably contracted this disease in the Tuli River a few months prior, just before heading to England to propose to Shirley. Shirley couldn't believe how much I slept.

I bought a classical nylon six-string guitar for Shirley to fuel her interest in playing the guitar. (Many years later, Shirley gifted this guitar to our daughter-in-law Jerrica, in the hopes that the gift would keep on giving. Jerrica sings like an angel. Carissia, our other daughter-in-law, is also an anointed singer.) We also did some shopping for items not readily available in Zimbabwe, such as sun-filtering curtains.

We headed "home" to Shabani after a glorious honeymoon and made school preparations. Shirley found a job at the local Central

African Building Society (CABS). She had previously worked in CABS in Bulawayo before emigrating to England.

Newlyweds

Shirley settled into her "new" home, town, job and church. She felt like a goldfish in a bowl, though. Everybody knew me, but everyone was still getting to know her. It was a big transition for Shirley, who had returned from England to marry me. She wondered what people's expectations were.

Shirley had received the Holy Spirit upon her conversion to Christ as a fifteen-year-old but had not yet received the baptism of the Holy Spirit with the accompanying gift of a heavenly language. Neil taught that we could receive the baptism of the Holy Spirit with the evidence of tongues—a heavenly language. Paul addresses this in 1 Corinthians 14: "*For he that speaketh in an unknown tongue speaketh not unto men, but unto God: for no man understandeth him; howbeit in the spirit he speaketh mysteries. … He that speaketh in an unknown tongue edifieth himself…I would that ye all spake with tongues…. For if I pray in an unknown tongue, my spirit prayeth…. I thank my God, I speak with tongues more than ye all*" (verses 2, 4–5, 14a, 18, KJV). All throughout the book of Acts, people received the baptism of the Holy Spirit with the evidence of tongues. Jesus Himself had the Holy Spirit come on Him in the form of a dove at His water baptism. I prayed quietly that Shirley would receive this same baptism gift. One Sunday morning, she did. Now we could both pray in English and the Holy Ghost (heavenly language). Little did we know that we would need this *dunamis* (dynamite) of the Holy Spirit as He continued to lead us in all the glorious things He had planned for our lives.

Promotion

A few months later I was invited to apply for the assistant headmaster's (principal's) position at Umniati (now Munyati) Primary (Elementary) about three and a half hours away. Normally one would need to serve for seven years as a teacher before applying for such a position. However, I was one of the few who had earned a four-year bachelor's degree in education (most earned a three-year certificate in education), plus there had been an exodus of professional and skilled workers, including headmasters, owing to the war. I was offered the position just before Christmas. Shirley and I packed and made moving arrangements. At just twenty-five years of age, I was promoted to the position of assistant headmaster and a year later was appointed as headmaster.

Underprivileged

My friend Ray, whom I'd last seen at the youth camp at the Tuli Circle in southeastern Zimbabwe, had introduced us to an opportunity to serve as leaders on holidays for underprivileged children. Shirley and I led three such holidays over the next almost three years, one while living in Shabani and two while living in Umniati. While living in Shabani, we flew over thirty children to Durban, South Africa, for an amazing beach holiday replete with fun games and Bible stories. While living in Umniati, we flew with another group of elementary-aged children to Simonstown, South Africa, for a week's holiday. Shirley's youngest sister, Lee, was not underprivileged but received permission to accompany us. She had a blast. Our last holiday with a group of children was to the Vumba (Bvumba) Mountains in the eastern highlands of Zimbabwe. Our heart was to minister Jesus to these children and to give them a holiday of a lifetime that they would long remember with fondness. It was hard work but so much fun!

Shirley and I had risen above the turbulence of our new life starting together. We'd risen *above the storms*. All seemed still. Then, almost imperceptibly, we spied dust and debris spinning in the distance....

Shirley's Reflections

Our life together in Africa was rich and full. Schools in Rhodesia began early in the morning and ended at one o'clock. That was the academic part of the day. The afternoons were for sports. Everyone had to participate at least two afternoons a week. As a child, I lived for sports and took part in activities every school day. Once married, we coached various school sports, such as swimming, field hockey, track events, soccer and tennis. Part of the teachers' training included all sports. Martin was also a certified tennis coach and lifeguard.

CHAPTER 5

Calling

(1982-1983)

Crisis Faced: Cross – Denying Self
Crisis: Listening – Your Will, Not Mine
Storm: Dust Devil – Small Whirlwinds

School Headmaster

I met the outgoing principal in the school office. Umniati (Munyati) Primary, a K-6 elementary school, was situated just off the narrow strip road that connected the small community to the main Harare-to-Bulawayo artery road. The nearest town, Que Que (now KweKwe, where my sister, Mary, was born), was about twenty-two miles away. The buildings were connected and elongated and faced the road. On the left side was the kindergarten through second-grade classroom. An adjoining music and assembly room was next. The third- through sixth-grade classroom was next with a small patio leading to the main school office. The school building was covered with corrugated metal roofing and sides and was not the most attractive facility. But it served its purpose of educating children from the local power station and the surrounding farmers' children. A metal overhang awning-type structure ran along the entire front of the building and provided shelter from storms. Immediately in front of the school and slightly to the right, as you faced the road, was a large mound covered with grass. I discovered that this was a bomb shelter bunker in case of a guerrilla-terrorist attack. Beyond the bunker was the school sports field.

"I'm in charge here. I give the orders..." started the outgoing principal before pausing momentarily, "...and I carry them out," he exclaimed, chuckling. In the next two years, I would find out how true those words were.

Power Station Community

Shirley and I were privileged to have quite a large brick home next door to the power station manager, compliments of the power station. We paid a mere twelve dollars per month for rent and utilities. Our home was just over a mile away from the school and located on the narrow tarred road that ran around the base of a hill, about a mile and a half in circumference. One had to peer through the bushes and trees on the front perimeter to see the house, which was set back about twenty-five yards. A screened-in porch ran the length of the house front. A steep stony driveway led to an open carport that stood to the right of the house. A narrow path snaked its way up the steep hill at the back of our home. Atop the hill stood an imposing clubhouse complete with private rooms, offices, a large dining hall, and a bar. To the back right of the clubhouse stood a beautifully manicured English bowling lawn. To the left, two squash courts were carved into the hillside. On top of the hill to the left of the clubhouse was a twenty-five-yard square pool with a diving board. To the far right of the clubhouse were two all-weather tennis courts. We paid a meagre twelve dollars per month to use all amenities. I was just twenty-five years of age and felt like a king.

The house had been vacant for a while and an airborne squadron of tiny fleas canvased the interior. While waiting for our furniture to arrive, we dined at the clubhouse. I recall Shirley and I sitting with some friendly folk and watching as fleas jettisoned across the table. Embarrassing. Scratch! Scratch! Our furniture and belongings were delivered, in part, by a removal company a few days after our arrival. Shirley's prized wedding dress, which she had purchased in England, and other items, plus a couch, were mysteriously missing. All my clothes and some of Shirley's were missing. Efforts to recoup our losses were futile since the government insurance claimed they had no money.

Stronger Together

The day before school started, the K-2nd grade teacher resigned. She was a farmer's wife and a trained teacher but for some reason decided not to teach. Shirley stepped in and filled the gap. A few weeks later she was officially observed teaching by a regional education official and was told she was doing a great job. Shirley was a natural teacher and structured. My part as principal and third- through sixth-grade teacher was to help with the lesson plans.

We look back on these days with mostly very fond memories. Shirley and I did everything together. We were still relatively newlyweds and traveled to school together (compliments of the power station bus), ate lunch together after school finished at 1:00 p.m., listened to faith-building audiotapes of preachers such as Fred Price and British Israeli preacher and educator Derek Prince, then went back to school for afternoon sports. We coached field hockey, soccer, athletics, cricket and swimming. We also produced a play called *The Music Machine*. Power station personnel rigged a borrowed "Music Machine" that whistled and shot out plumes of "white smoke." The play was based on the nine fruits of the Spirit from Galatians 5:22–23 in the Bible and was our way of sharing the gospel with our students and community: *"But the fruit of the Spirit is love, joy, peace, forbearance, kindness, goodness, faithfulness, gentleness and self-control. Against such things there is no law"* (NIV). We rehearsed at school for months and then moved to the hall at the clubhouse for several practices. We ran the musical for two nights and drew capacity crowds from the local and surrounding community.

Shirley and I also rented a monthly Christian movie from the capital city of Harare and showed it free of charge in the clubhouse hall. The bar was the focus of attention, so we invited everyone to come in and watch the movie, beers and all—anything to get the gospel out. We also lead a weekly Bible study at our home. This study was taking off with several of our neighbors attending until a visiting and somewhat overzealous and insensitive "full gospel" individual burst into "tongues" and shocked the unchurched audience, who never returned. This still saddens me.

I was a Christian principal, and we ran the local government school on Christian principles. We would start each day with a short chapel, singing and prayer. God's presence was tangible at times. This was mostly well received by the community, but one parent objected to her child being indoctrinated with myths and fairy tales. Ironically, this lady had stood in as secretary when my first secretary had stepped down to help her husband, a local farmer. The first secretary was amazing and had college-age children. We became fast friends and enjoyed playing tennis at the weekends. Thankfully, she returned as a full-time secretary with coaxing.

Parent Attack

One day I heard a commotion towards Shirley's classroom. I peeked out the door and saw the former stand-in secretary and another mother, both oversized buxom ladies, pounding on Shirley's classroom door. Slight Shirley was on the other side holding the door handle up but only by the strength of God. Just one of these brute ladies could have easily flattened Shirley in an instant. She called out to her class to be super quiet and assured them that everything would be all right. In the meantime, my attempts at dissuading the ladies from their hostilities were futile and met with loud threats of lawsuits if I laid hands on them.

Apparently one mother had a question about the Parent Teacher Association (PTA) monies. My wife directed them to the former stand-in secretary as she kept the money. This infuriated the stand-in, who thought Shirley was accusing her of stealing the money. She had made no such accusation. Eventually the pounding on the door stopped and the "ladies" slumped off quite dissatisfied. I breathed a huge sigh of relief. *Thank You, Jesus.*

Community Thief

One night Shirley and I were in bed. We'd locked up as normal and left the keys in the doors, but Shirley had left a side kitchen window open for an area cat to gain entry to some food and milk. I awoke earlier than Shirley and found that the door leading into the kitchen was locked. I called out to Shirley and asked her if she had locked this door. She assured me that she had not. Shirley then discovered a burnt-out match on her bedside table. She checked her handbag and discovered that the six dollars she'd had was missing. I went out the front door and circled back to the back door and found it open. The thief had made good his escape. The thief, a neighbor's local African helper, was apprehended a few days later. We found out that he had visited neighbors across the road on the same night that he visited us. He had helped himself to a beer from their refrigerator and a banana. We were so thankful for God's divine protection and unusual deep sleep, especially for Shirley, who was a particularly light sleeper.

School Integration

The War for Independence in Rhodesia lasted from July 1964 to December 1979. The quest was for blacks to take control of the country from the ruling white minority. This was a bloody war with barbarous acts of terrorism to achieve the end goal. After the war, former freedom fighters, otherwise known as terrorists by the white minority, were reassigned to militia duties such as guarding railway lines and important power installations. The early 1980s also saw the integration of schools in the newly named nation of Zimbabwe. Shirley and I welcomed all students with open arms, white and black. The younger black students in Shirley's K-2 class spoke little to no English. Most of the older students in my class could speak a little English. Typically, the black students would honor us as teachers by kneeling at our desks and casting their gaze downwards. This act was a sign of respect in African culture.

Shirley fell in love with all her students. She lovingly recalls one five-year-old African boy, Tikawa, who had large, intelligent, mischievous brown eyes and was eager to learn. Such was the joy that our students brought to our hearts. We loved them, and they loved us. One of Shirley's students moved to a large school in the nearby town of Kwe Kwe. At that time, students were ranked by their performance on end-of-term exams. To Shirley's credit, this young girl was the top student in her much larger urban class. Shirley was an excellent teacher! And she loved her principal!

Shirley and I spent our evenings learning keywords and phrases of the African Shona language. For example, "Mangwanani, Mufundisi," was translated as "Good morning, Teacher" (literally, pastor). We labeled our posters in English and Shona and called on those who could speak English to translate for those who could not.

Our students especially enjoyed the monthly field trips to such places as local farms, a cotton farm, a ginnery, a clothing factory and a bank. The trips were well planned, and students were assigned before, during and after activities to ensure they grasped the key concepts. Back in the classroom, the field trips lent themselves to integration with writing, math, reading, spelling, history, science and art. The integrated learning approach worked well with our field trips. We also had more teacher-directed learning, especially in the "three Rs" of reading, writing and arithmetic (math). The joy of learning!

Most African students were eager learners and picked up English quite readily. By the end of the second year, they were some of the top students and were awarded prizes for achievement and progress. This caused some of the white parents to refer to us as African lovers, except they used a derogatory term. We were not deterred. A local farmer's renegade grown son reportedly ran one of our older African female students off the road with his pickup truck. She had just recovered from a broken leg and reinjured it. It was quite likely that he was drinking. Sadly, nothing could be proven, and no charges were filed. Shirley and I visited the student in a hospital in Harare and brought her a little gift. She was overjoyed. A few months later she was back in school.

Speak to the Wind

We often held school galas in the local pool. On one occasion, a college friend of mine who was nicknamed "Nippy" came with a busload of students from Somabhula where I had gone to school as a child. This was about a two-hour trip one way. The gala was about to begin when low-rolling thunderclouds and heavy winds suddenly assailed us. Deck chairs were whipped up and dashed into the pool. The heavens opened. Nippy and I stood together and rebuked the storm and wind in Jesus' name. Almost immediately, the raging storm quieted, and the thunderous clouds rolled back, revealing the warm African sunshine. We discovered that the Bible is true. There really is power in agreement. "*How could one have chased a thousand, and two have put ten thousand to flight, unless their Rock had sold them, and the Lord had given them up?"* (Deuteronomy 32:30, ESV).

The chairman of the local PTA was a local tomato farmer who sold his produce internationally. He also helped us design a very productive school vegetable garden. He came weekly and instructed us on the art of growing all kinds of vegetables. We also used the school bunker to propagate mushrooms at the suggestion of Shirley's mother. Each student had a veggie patch and delighted in looking after his or her garden. A high-wire fence surrounded the garden behind the school. This kept most deer out but not the occasional monkey. The students sold their produce to the local community and raised funds for the school.

The night before another school gala, I was meeting at the clubhouse with the PTA. "There is a phone call for you," the waiter interrupted and said to the chairman. He left and was absent for some time. He returned ashen. His farm manager had just been shot through the mouth by the local militia (former guerrilla-terrorists) who were supposed to be protecting the power station. This was a major blow to us and our tight-knit community. We strongly considered canceling the gala scheduled for the following day, but the farmer, a strong supporter of the school, opted to continue. I remember his son Graham swimming heroically through cascading tears of grief. All the students were deeply affected. We lost the swimming gala.

James Saved
Shirley and I had purchased my dad's black motorcycle. It was a small bike less than 100cc but had just enough "oomph" to make it to the top of the clubhouse hill. We had just disembarked from the bike on one occasion when we heard a shrill scream coming from the pool. A young girl had found James, an African clubhouse waiter, in the deep end of the pool. She had jumped in and dragged him to the side. My British Red Cross training and Shirley's nursing kicked in. We ran to the edge, grasped James under his arms, and hauled him out. I rolled him on his stomach and pushed firmly between his shoulders to squeeze out any pool water. Shirley knelt by my side ready to use her nursing skills. After a few back pushes, James sputtered and gasped for breath. The local

power station ambulance was soon on the scene, and I accompanied James to the nearest hospital over twenty miles away, praying all the way. James made a full recovery.

Prayer Effects

One school mom told me about a home situation and wondered if I could help. The lights were coming on at night by themselves, and bed-covers were being ripped from their bed. The lady had been to our home Bible studies and knew about the power of prayer. I told her that my wife and I would come and pray. We anointed the home with oil and prayed prayers of deliverance, commanding all demons to leave. We'd never done this before, but we knew we had authority as believers and that Jesus commanded demons to leave. We prayed in bold faith. The demons left, and the family never had a reoccurrence of demonic activity. *"I have given you authority to trample on snakes and scorpions and to overcome all the power of the enemy; nothing will harm you"* (Luke 10:19, NIV). *Thank You, Jesus!*

One farmer's wife who had a daughter at our school told us that it looked like they had lost their wheat crop due to excessive rains. Shirley and I immediately prayed. Later that day, we discovered Psalm 81:16, which states, *"But you would be fed with the finest of wheat; with honey from the rock I would satisfy you"* (NIV). We staked our faith in God's Word. The rain stopped, and the farmer's wheat was saved. Hallelujah! *Thank You, Jesus!*

Parasitic Miracle Cure

I was teaching my students about the necessity to have a bilharzia test if they had been in any rivers or lakes. Schistosomiasis, the scientific name, is caused by parasitic flatworms that burrow through your skin and lay eggs in your bloodstream. The effects are often fatigue, blood in stool and urine, headaches and so on. Blindness, deafness and even death can result if the disease is not treated. It suddenly dawned on me that I was being hypocritical.

Prior to going overseas to ask Shirley to marry me, I had gone on that church youth camp hundreds of miles into the African bush to the Tuli Circle. It was the exact location where the early pioneers had set up camp with their ox wagons in the 1890s. We slept on the banks of the Tuli River underneath the sparkling stars and planned to hike to the other side of the river in the morning. This meant fording a one-hundred-yard flooding river and dodging the large cow paddies being washed down from higher ground. We also had to keep an eye out for crocodiles and hippos.

We forged the river going single file. The river was up to our necks in places, but we made it safely to the other side where we discovered evidence of the early pioneers, including "bully-beef" tins with half the bully-beef dried up still inside, pieces of green bottles, and gun shells. There was also a local cemetery. One story was told of a pioneer who felt an animal brush against him in the dark. He thought it was his dog and bent down to pet it. Unfortunately, it was a lion—hence the gravestone. What a sad demise. It was this story that flashed through my mind as I was strongly urging my students to be tested for this waterborne, debilitating and potentially fatal disease of bilharzia. I had also gone fishing with my pastor friend and stood waist-deep in dam water. Ironically, as a child and youth, I had veered away from immersion in rivers and lakes because of this disease. Now as a young teacher and principal, I let my guard down. There was just too much fun to be had.

I decided to take my own advice and had blood drawn at the local clinic. Unfortunately, they lost the blood, and I had to have it drawn again. I thought this might have been just "punishment" for my lack of faith, as I had previously prayed against bilharzia. The results came back negative. The local nurse said, "You had bilharzia, and the treatment you had cured you." The telltale signs of dead bilharzia eggs were evident.

I retorted, "I have never had medical treatment for bilharzia."

The nurse was quite insistent. "The results show that you had bilharzia and that the treatment worked. You no longer have bilharzia." I responded that I had prayed, and it was evident that God had healed me. I don't think she was convinced.

Bird of Prey

On Sundays, we drove in our red German-made combi-camper van (with the steering on the opposite side to our normal) to a small Pentecostal church in Kwekwe (formerly Que Que) about forty minutes away.

The services were intimate and allowed for participation and exercise of spiritual gifts and preaching. John Henson, the pastor, had been my senior at high school. I knew the entire family. They were all strong believers in Christ. John would faithfully visit us on his motorcycle once a month, and the church would occasionally travel to our home, where we enjoyed food and sweet fellowship.

We heard about a visiting South African evangelist who would be ministering at Redcliff, a small iron-mining town near Kwekwe, where our pastor, John, and his wife, Clare, lived. Shirley and I decided to attend the service slated for a Saturday evening. I played the guitar for the worship part of the service. Suddenly, without warning, the pastor swiveled and locked eyes with me. "God has called you to follow Him. You know what you must do. Do it." That was the word. I knew exactly what he meant and what the Lord was saying through him.

Neil, the pastor friend who had married us in Shabani, had emigrated to America. He was the pastor of a non-denominational church that had a Christian school. He had invited us by letter *three times* to come over and join him in the ministry. Since we were still newlyweds, we decided to stay for two years in Umniati (Munyati) to strengthen our marriage bonds. Scripture reinforced this for us: "*For **two** whole years Paul stayed there in his own rented house and welcomed all who came to see him*" (Acts 28:30, NIV, emphasis added). We felt God was telling us through this and one other verse to remain in Umniati for two years. We felt a strong tug toward America but realized the "cost" of leaving our parents, siblings and the land we loved. Plus, Shirley had previously emigrated to England, and this would mean another transatlantic move.

The next morning during my devotional Bible reading and prayer time, the Spirit of God spoke powerfully to me through Isaiah 46:11, confirming the evangelist's word and what I was sensing in my spirit. It was as though God was standing in America and calling to me. "*From the east I summon a **bird of prey**; from a far-off land, a man to fulfill my purpose. What I have said, that I will bring about; what I have planned, that I will do*" (NIV, emphasis added). In subsequent months, Shirley and I took half a term's leave plus the upcoming one-month school vacation time, a total of eleven weeks. We did a continental European trip, going from England to Belgium, to Holland, down the Rhine River in

Germany, through Switzerland and up through France before heading back to England. Then we boarded a flight to Sioux Falls, South Dakota, in the United States. We stayed with Neil and his wife Noline and their children and holidayed with them in the Black Hills. We also became acquainted with the church and Christian school. The principal's position that I was originally asked to fill had been taken, but there was still a need for teachers.

Confirming "Words"

One evening while we were attending a small group Bible study with Neil and Noline in the nearby town of Canton, South Dakota, a lady had a vision that she felt applied to me. "I see a golden sphere and keys. You are to choose the golden sphere." Ordinarily, this would not mean anything to me or anyone else perhaps, but I was still seeking God's continued confirmation about coming to America. I immediately understood how this vision applied to me. The sphere represented the Kingdom of God and His will for my life. The keys represented promotion and opportunity. In Zimbabwe, there was ample opportunity for rapid promotion in schools, especially since many principals were leaving the country for political and economic reasons. This "word" was further confirmation to me that God wanted me in America. Shirley wept the night through. She feared leaving her homeland for the second time in just a few years. Why hadn't God spoken to her?

A lady at the Canton meeting invited Shirley to a Women's Aglow ladies-only meeting scheduled in the next few days. The speaker had a "word" for Shirley: "I have seen your tears. I have heard your cries. Do not be afraid to do what God has called you to do." In an instant, Shirley's tearful disposition disappeared, and she resumed her normal upbeat cheerful self. God had spoken to Shirley, and her heart was again full of joy. "… *This is what the Lord, the God of your father David, says: I have heard your prayer and seen your tears; I will heal you. On the third day from now you will go up to the temple of the Lord*'" (2 Kings 20:5, NIV).

Africa Return and America Preparations

We returned to Zimbabwe, handed in our notice for the end of the year, then packed up, sold up and gave things away. Our decision to leave the school and go to America did not augur well with students' parents, especially the white parents. They had already experienced an interim African principal for a couple of months while Shirley and I visited America. The substitute African teacher for Shirley's class did not speak good English. She reportedly would hold up items such as a pair of shorts and say to the children, "This is a shots," instead of "This is a pair of shorts." The white parents saw the school as going downhill. Some of the black parents may have felt this way, too, although they never expressed it. This period of integration in schools was new for everybody.

I recall asking the interim African principal if a golf course had opened in the community as I saw golf clubs behind the office door. (I knew there was no golf club in the community.) He quickly replied, "These are for the parents. They are so angry." Part of this anger was cast on us now that we were leaving. Fortunately, the good graces of the community mostly returned when we spoke with them individually, sharing how God had called us to America. One lady even came to our home and kissed me goodbye on the cheek. It was sad to leave this tight-knit community.

Timely Provision

Three weeks before our departure, we still did not have the airfare to America. However, we had the confident assurance that the God who had called us would make a way. As one popular quote (often attributed to John Wesley) reminded us, "Faith is not believing God can. It is knowing that He will." Or as the Bible puts it in Hebrews 11:1, "*Now faith is the substance* [realization] *of things hoped for, the evidence* [confidence] *of things not seen*" (NKJV). One week later, we were visiting our Redcliff pastor, who had now moved to Harare. He needed a vehicle, and we needed the airfare. We "sold" and "sowed" the vehicle to our pastor, who took over the payments. (Amazingly, John witnessed about Jesus to the elderly couple to whom he made the payments. Both experienced a glorious transaction with their Savior—and just in time, for the husband died two days later.) God's perfect timing. We paid for our tickets and had a small amount of cash remaining. We then cleared all our emigration responsibilities. On January 17, 1984, we flew to Shirley's sister in Johannesburg, South Africa. We landed at Chicago O'Hare's

International Airport ten days later, on January 27, my brother Brian's birthday. Little did we know that the struggles and trials to this point were merely training ground for what lay ahead. *Goodbye, Africa! Welcome to America!*

We had risen *above the storms* of departure and unknowingly headed blindly into hazardous and icy conditions....

Shirley's Reflections

Our house in Umniati, Zimbabwe, was twenty-two miles from the nearest town. On Friday, we received our monthly salary in cash. On Sunday, we drove to town for church. It was there I gave our salary to our pastor's wife, Clare, to bank for us the following day. That evening was the night of our break-in. The thief didn't get away with much. We found Martin's briefcase and my purse on the kitchen table. I only had six dollars left in my purse. God had intervened for us yet again.

CHAPTER 6

Welcome to America!

(1984)

Crisis Faced: Visa – Permission to Enter
Crisis: Loneliness – Making Friends
Storm: Ice Storm – Dangerous Driving Conditions

O'Hare Interrogation

Shirley and I had flown from Zimbabwe to South Africa on January 17, 1984. We stayed with Shirley's sister Jane and her husband, Ken, near Pretoria for several days before boarding a flight to Brussels, Belgium, where we stayed the night in the airport hotel. The next morning, we boarded a Sabena Airlines flight to the United States. A flight steward approached us and told us we had been bumped up to first class. *Thank You, Jesus.* We were so excited. We'd given up, sold up and packed up, and now we were on our way to join our pastor and friend from Zvishavane (Shabani), Zimbabwe, in a full-time Christian school ministry in Sioux Falls, South Dakota. The giant 747 touched down on time at Chicago's O'Hare International Airport several hours later on the afternoon of January 27, my now late brother Brian's birthday.

We shuffled our way to passport control. We understood from a friend that the maximum length of the visa was nine months, so that is what we requested. However, instead of granting the visas, the officer grilled us with all kinds of questions and wanted to know why we were coming into the country. We told him. He then drilled down on why we only had $300. We explained that Zimbabwe restricted foreign currency to $300. We also explained that we were being sponsored by a church. When pressed further about finances, I jokingly quipped that I would "sing for my supper." Bad timing! The officer excused himself but returned several minutes later and escorted us to an immigration room.

The immigration interrogation room was painted gray and had bare concrete block walls. On the far side of the room sat a stout female immigration official. Stoic. She did not smile. She motioned for us to sit on the two wooden chairs on the far side of her desk. The passport official clicked the door behind us. My heart was racing. This didn't look good. Plus, the clock was ticking before our next flight. I glanced at my watch. The sole departing flight to our Sioux Falls, South Dakota, destination was set to leave in just over two hours.

The questioning barrage started like a machine gun with a finger stuck on the trigger. Whoa! This was serious. "Why are you here? You're trying to emigrate illegally. Where's your money?" We sat composed but shocked. Non-reactive. We measured our responses deliberately and truthfully.

"We're being sponsored by a church in Sioux Falls. We are here to serve in a Christian school," I explained. I even produced a cover letter from the Sioux Falls church on their letterhead explaining that they were sponsoring us in America. However, the immigration officer "pooh-poohed" the letter. She left her office momentarily and returned a few minutes later and stated that the church did not corroborate our story. (Later we found out from the church that they had received no such call.) The badgering and barrage of questions continued unabated. We felt like Moses facing the Red Sea with the Egyptians behind. There was no way of escape...but God. *"There hath no temptation taken you but such as is common to man: but God is faithful, who will not suffer you to be tempted above that ye are able; but will with the temptation also make a way to escape, that ye may be able to bear it"* (1 Corinthians 10:13, KJV). The two-hour window was rapidly narrowing. Now there were only minutes left before the only departing Northwest Airlines flight to Sioux Falls, South Dakota, took off.

Angelic Intervention

There was a sharp knock on the solid wooden door. "Come in," barked the disgruntled immigration officer, obviously not happy about a disturbance. We were prey in her talons, and she was ready for the "kill." Of course, the officer was doing her job, but it was hard to see how "all things were working together for our good," as Romans 8:28 says, yet in retrospect they were. A Sabena Belgian Airlines employee entered with a command presence.

"These people need to be on the Northwest flight to Sioux Falls, and they are leaving now. I'm here to escort them to the plane. Thank you for releasing them now." He spoke with authority and confident insistence. He was firm, professional and polite, the consummate professional. The immigration officer seemed flustered and unsure of what to do. She confiscated our passports and stamped them. We were given a ten-day visa and ordered to appear before the immigration authorities in St. Paul-Minneapolis.

The Sabina employee led us out of the office and to the Sioux Falls departure gate. Our baggage was checked in. Everyone had boarded. There was not a soul in sight. Just before descending the walkway onto the plane, I glanced over my shoulder. No one was there. Where was the "man" who had delivered us to this plane? He must be somewhere. How could he just vanish? I suspended that thought momentarily and hurriedly found my seat. Later I reflected on what had happened and realized that God had sent angelic intervention to help us through our impossible trial. Why would a man in a Sabena Airlines uniform escort us to our Northwest Airline departure gate, especially when we had disembarked two hours previously? How could he have known we were undergoing interrogation? *"Be not forgetful to entertain strangers: for thereby some have entertained angels unawares"* (Hebrews 13:2, KJV). *"Many are the afflictions of the righteous, but the Lord delivers him out of them all"* (Psalm 34:19, NKJV).

Sioux Falls, South Dakota

A couple of hours later the plane banked to the right. Far below were the welcoming, twinkling lights of our new home, Sioux Falls, South Dakota. The abdomen-like blow that we'd received in Chicago was replaced with a fast-rising barometer of joy. Somehow, God had made a way thus far. Somehow, He would continue to make a way. *"Then Samuel took a stone and set it up between Mizpah and Shen, and called its name Ebenezer, saying, 'Thus far the Lord has helped us'"* (1 Samuel 7:12, NKJV).

We were warmly greeted at the Sioux Falls airport by Neil and his wife, Noline (our pastors from Zimbabwe, who had moved to America), and a welcoming committee comprised of church members and school parents. Neil had invited us to America to join him in full-time ministry. Initially I was offered the principal's position, but since we delayed two years in Zimbabwe, the position had been filled. I was now coming to serve as a second- and third-grade combination teacher in the church school. An overarching banner was strung from the airport ceiling with the ornate and brightly colored words, "Martin and Shirley, Welcome to Victory Academy!"

The Chicago heaviness was replaced with gladness and joy. Our spirits bubbled up like water in a fizzy fountain. Once outside the airport and while boarding a vehicle, we experienced a bitter Arctic chill. We left Africa in 98° weather (Fahrenheit) and arrived in South Dakota with a windchill temperature of minus 40° Fahrenheit. Nothing could have prepared us for the temperature difference, but we were soon whisked away in a 1976 Grand LeMans to our "little house on the prairie"—a small white cottage at 1534 South "Prairie," Sioux Falls. The car handled so smoothly that it felt like we were driving on ice. We probably were.

Welcome Provision

The church congregation, along with Neil (the pastor), had furbished the cottage entirely. The freezer and pantry were fully stocked. We had basic furniture and even a waterbed—all items donated by church members. We did not have to purchase anything. People stayed briefly to see our joyous response and then hurried out the door. After all, there was church the next day, Sunday. Neil and Noline were the last to leave. They again expressed their gratitude for our joining them in the ministry. As they were leaving, Neil held out some car keys and dropped them in my hand. "The Grand LeMans is yours!" he exclaimed. We couldn't believe our ears. We had sown our combi vehicle at half-price to a pastor friend in Zimbabwe and now God was blessing us "immeasurably more" with this incredible vehicle. *"Now unto him that is able to do exceeding abundantly above all that we ask or think, according to the power that worketh in us"* (Ephesians 3:20, KJV). We slept like newborns in the warm waterbed.

Driving in America

The Grand LeMans had been parked at the side of our cottage. We rose the next morning and readied ourselves for church. We wanted to leave in plenty of time since this was our first Sunday. Then I saw it. A white blanket of snow covered our vehicle. I dressed as warmly as I could and set out to brush the snow off the vehicle. Brushing fresh white snow was easy enough, but it was the thick ice on the windshield that baffled me. I tried scraping the ice with a scraper to no avail. I realized that hot water may crack the windshield, so I applied tepidly warm water with a cloth. It took several minutes of elbow grease, scouring small circles, before the ice gradually thinned and I could see the windshield. Fortunately, the windshield was still intact. No cracks from the lukewarm water. Good. I continued the circular motion for another few minutes until I had a porthole-sized circular clearing.

The vehicle started without a hitch, but then I had the challenge of backing it out onto the road in front of our cottage. No problem. I could manage that. I had already been introduced to American driving conditions several months prior when we had visited Neil and Noline on a scouting visit. I had driven their large American vehicle filled with joyful talkative ladies, children and a dog. At that time driving on the left side of the road was new for me, and I had to consciously think about which side of the road I should end up on, especially when turning corners. With lots of encouragement, I drove everyone to our destination, a bank where we needed to cash a traveler's check.

"Speak to the pole," Noline instructed. "Tell it what you want."

"The pole?" I inquired. "Are you sure?" (We didn't speak to poles in Africa, except at a drive-in cinema.)

"Speak to it," she urged.

I plucked up the courage and mustered up my most articulate "Prince Charles" (now King Charles) accent. "Good afternoon. Please could you help me cash a traveler's check? Thank you."

"What? What do you want?" the teller spat out between gum chewing. I tried again, but to no avail.

"Huh? You want to do what?" Chew. Chew.

The ladies in the car collapsed in stitches. My "Prince Charles" accent was not being understood. Finally, one of the American ladies translated. "He wants to cash a check," she drawled.

The money came flying back through an opaque tube. I ducked subconsciously, fearing some flying object was about to crash into my skull. But then the money holder in the tube slowed and deposited into the exit sleeve. I retrieved the money—plus suckers for the children and a treat for the dog. My face gave away my incredulity, and the occupants collapsed again in laughter. What a learning experience. At least I was learning to drive an automatic vehicle in America—on the "wrong" side of the road for me.

I recalled this first driving encounter as I gently pressed the accelerator on the Grand LeMans. Instead of backing nicely down the short driveway to the road, the back wheels started spinning and the car fishtailed toward the cottage. Oh no. There was little room to spare—three feet perhaps—and now there was less space. I gently squeezed the accelerator and then backed off. I did this repeatedly to gently rock the vehicle with the hopes that it would gain traction and move forward. In all, it took me thirty minutes of rocking and sliding ever closer to the side of the cottage before I successfully backed out into the road. The cottage was damage-free. *Thank You, Jesus.* Now I faced the drive on snow-covered roads where I would be driving on the "wrong" side of the road with unfamiliar road signs covered with snow. Talk about hyperventilation! We made it forty minutes late to our first church service but still received a warm welcome and introduction.

Visa Granted

The following week, the pastor and one other elder, plus Shirley and I, made the almost 300-mile trip to the immigration office in St. Paul-Minneapolis. The immigration officer immediately understood our position and granted us a one-year visa. In retrospect, if we had come in under our own human wisdom and been granted just nine months for our visa, we would have been returned to Zimbabwe (more about that later).

"Trust in the Lord with all thine heart; and lean not unto thine own under-standing. In all thy ways acknowledge him, and he shall direct thy paths" (Proverbs 3:5–6, KJV).

God's mighty angel brought us through the initial entry storm and helped us *soar above the storms* in our early days in America. Then the winds picked up. Intense weather was forecast....

Shirley's Reflections

Moving to America was a huge undertaking. I had already left Rhodesia once when I emigrated to England. Just over two years later, I went back to Rhodesia (then Zimbabwe) to marry Martin. I knew what it was like to leave family and friends and immerse oneself in a new culture. How-ever, I believed that God had called us to America, and I wanted to be obedient. Not my will, but His. Even the weather was starkly different. I didn't like the bitter cold or snow. But God was always there to warm my heart, as was my husband.

CHAPTER 7

Far From Home

(1984-1986)

Crisis Faced: Culture Shock – Disorientation
Crisis: Identity – How Do We Fit In?
Storm: Squall Line – Severe Line of Thunderstorms

Car Deliverance

I immediately "jumped" into ministry. I taught a combination second- and third-grade class in the church school. Shirley stayed home and adjusted to life alone in America. On our fourteenth day in America, we were driving back from a grocery store where we'd noticed "coupon specials." This sounded like a deal to our thrifty Zimbabwean way of thinking where deals were rare, so we made the trek across town. Later we discovered that "special deals" were not necessarily special and were very common in America.

It was about 9:00 p.m. and dark as we were returning home. The highways were covered with compacted snow. When crossing an overpass, I noticed a sign with an arrow and bump. I did not realize that I was now on a divided three-lane highway with one-way traffic. I was still expecting to see traffic coming towards me. Strangely, there was no traffic. I stayed in the middle lane, surmising that this was a "snow road" where two lanes went one direction with one lane going the other. I was still becoming accustomed to the driving conditions in wintry Sioux Falls. There's no snow in Zimbabwe. I saw our street name, "Prairie," signaled quickly, checked that there was no oncoming traffic, then made a left turn—right into the path of a state penitentiary van traveling a little behind me but in the left lane. Kaboom! The large van crashed violently into the rear driver's side door and catapulted the huge Grand LeMans across the highway. We spun 180°, hit the curb forcefully, and then bounced back with a shocking jolt that banged me on the left side of the head. Shirley was unharmed. We were now facing the opposite direction.

The V8 engine stalled. Shirley bolted out of the passenger side and ran to a neighbor's house for help. I sat in stony silence. Then I peered out the driver's window. An oversized penitentiary officer was stomping toward me. I could hear the threatening "crunch, crunch" of his hobnail boots on the compressed snow. This was it. I hung my head low waiting for the final blow, unable to escape from the vehicle. My right hand gently pressed the growing lump on my head. The crunching stopped.

"You okay?" a man's gruff voice inquired. I sensed what I thought might be a sliver of concern for my well-being. I cashed in…

"I think so," I responded hesitantly. "I just have a lump on my head…"

"Don't worry about the accident. We can easily replace vehicles but not people." What amazing words of comfort, grace and forgiveness all in one sentence. I thanked the man for his kindness and explained that we were new to America and driving on snowy roads. "*And be kind to one another, tenderhearted, forgiving one another, even as God in Christ forgave you*" (Ephesians 4:32, NKJV).

Soon the "blue light" of a police vehicle lit up the night sky, and I found myself sitting in the back of the car. From my British Red Cross experience, I knew that I was in shock, and from watching occasional American "whodunits," I realized that everything I said could and would be used against me in a court of law. My responses to the cop's questions were therefore meditatively slow like molasses and highly contemplative. I told the truth. The cop heard my accent and was seemingly sympathetic to my plight. Later a judge fined me just twenty-five dollars for an improper left turn but ordered me to pay for the repairs on the state penitentiary van. No jail time. *Thank You, Jesus!*

Prior to the accident, Shirley and I had inquired about insurance coverage for the Grand LeMans. However, insurance companies required a South Dakota driver's license. We had international drivers' licenses. It would take time, preparation and money to secure our South Dakota license. This "narrow escape" made this need our continuing top priority.

We didn't know it at the time, but Shirley was newly pregnant with our firstborn son, Timothy. The enemy had tried to "steal" our lives and that of our firstborn. Timothy has grown to be a man of God with fierce faith who contends for the Kingdom of God. *"Because he has set his love upon Me, therefore I will deliver him; I will set him on high, because he has known My name. He shall call upon Me, and I will answer him; I will be with him in trouble; I will deliver him and honor him. With long life I will satisfy him, and show him My salvation"* (Psalm 91:14–16, NKJV).

Culture Shock

In the ensuing weeks, Shirley cleaned houses to help defray accident costs. Later she taught pre-school for a season at the church school. I was so proud of my dear wife. House cleaning was generally relegated to the "servants" in Africa, but we soon learned that "we" were the "servants" in America. At one home, Shirley did the washing, ironing and all cleaning, plus she looked after four kids under ten years of age with the dogs running in and out of the house. We also "babysat" for one doctor and his wife who went on vacation. In a couple of months, we had earned only $700, a paltry amount compared to the estimated $7,000-plus that was needed to repair the state penitentiary van and our own vehicle, which was considered written off but still drivable. This was way more than my first year's offerings of $4,500 for teaching in the church school. This was a heavy burden on us. We were new, in a strange country, dealing with ice and snow, driving on the "wrong" side of the road, facing huge changes in using the Abeka Christian curriculum (especially in a multi-grade classroom), plus becoming accustomed to a new church and completely different way of life. And Shirley was at home *alone* when she was not working. I had the car.

One day after Shirley obtained her South Dakota driver's license, she drove to the hospital for a pregnancy checkup. She parked on the side of the road but came back to see a ticket on her windshield. She was not a happy camper. The Roads Department had switched signs in Shirley's absence for snow-plowing reasons. We were still becoming accustomed to the alternate snow-plowing days. Shortly after the ticket, Shirley appeared before a judge. She had hardly spoken in response to the judge's question about what happened when the judge abruptly held up his hand and crisply stated, "No snow in Zimbabwe. Case dismissed." Shirley was over the moon and bought ice cream cones to celebrate. She then surprised me at the school with the good news and a cone. *Jesus, our Deliverer, we thank You.* "*You are my hiding place; You shall preserve me from trouble; You shall surround me with songs of deliverance. Selah*" (Psalm 32:7, NKJV).

I awoke early one morning about three months after the car accident. As I was reading God's Word and praying (which was and is my morning discipline), I distinctly heard the inner audible voice of the Holy Spirit: "*You won't have to pay another penny.*" At first I thought this was my own natural thinking, but the message conveyed was impressive and persistent. God's peace flooded my soul. I knew it was the Holy Spirit. I shared this with Shirley when she awoke.

I said, "Honey, I don't believe we are going to pay another penny toward our car debt. I believe God has completely taken care of it."

Shirley was incredulous at first since this did not make sense. How could our debt possibly be paid? That Sunday, an "anonymous" donor took care of the total amount owed toward the state penitentiary van. We continued to drive our Grand LeMans as is. The driver's door could only be opened from the outside, so when driving alone, I had to disembark from the front passenger door. We taped clear plastic over the left passenger window. "*And my God shall supply all your need according to His riches in glory by Christ Jesus*" (Philippians 4:19, NKJV). We were learning the powerful lesson that the little we give to Jesus is much in the Kingdom. "*Jesus replied, 'They do not need to go away. You give them something to eat.' 'We have here only five loaves of bread and two fish,' they answered. 'Bring them here to me,' he said. And he directed the people to sit down on the grass. Taking the five loaves and the two fish and looking up to heaven, he gave thanks and broke the loaves. Then he gave them to the disciples, and the disciples gave them to the people. They all ate and were satisfied, and the disciples picked up twelve basketfuls of broken pieces that were left over. The number of those who ate was about five thousand men, besides women and children"* (Matthew 14:16–21, NIV).

Residency Trials

Shortly after we arrived in America, we completed our application to become residents. This is not a given for anyone. However, we had been very diligent in our visit to Neil the previous year to find out exactly what we would need to become legal residents in America. Afterwards we had gone back to Zimbabwe and obtained letterhead copies of verifications from our bank, pastor and others of influence confirming the type of activity in which we were involved in Zimbabwe. These letters plus an accompanying letter of verification from the Sioux Falls church were part of the support materials in our residency application. A few months later, we received a letter from the immigration officials requesting that we submit the same support materials that we had already submitted. This was confusing and frustrating—another trial of our faith—but we resubmitted everything. A few months later we were summoned to the immigration office in St. Paul-Minneapolis. *"For we do not wrestle against flesh and blood, but against principalities, against powers, against the rulers of the darkness of this age, against spiritual hosts of wickedness in the heavenly places"* (Ephesians 6:12, NKJV).

We made the almost 300-mile trek from Sioux Falls, South Dakota, to St. Paul-Minneapolis, Minnesota. The wheels of the Grand LeMans were still turning despite the damaged bodywork. We arrived at the immigration office and approached the official at the counter. He quizzed us and told us we would have to return to Africa and apply for residency. Back to Africa?! Our world shattered. Shirley was pregnant with our firstborn, Timothy. We would have to make almost immediate arrangements to return to Zimbabwe since international airlines would not permit Shirley to fly later due to her being in the third trimester of pregnancy. Bewildered and frustrated, we decided to *"count it all joy"* (James 1:2, NKJV) and give thanks to God. Then we decided to celebrate the seemingly gargantuan setback with a Chinese lunch. God was in control, and the One who had called us would lead us. *"He who calls you is faithful, who also will do it"* (1 Thessalonians 5:24, NKJV). We have continued celebrations over the years but don't always wait for a crisis.

Back in Sioux Falls, we gleaned counsel from the pastor and church elders. They advised us to contact the local state senator, Larry Pressler. His office was very helpful and directed us to resubmit our application. We did. In the meantime, Larry Pressler contacted the immigration authorities on our behalf.

Meanwhile, our visa time in the States was fast ebbing away. Part of the immigration requirement was a medical screening. I passed mine, but Shirley showed up positive for tuberculosis (TB). It was a too critical time in the pregnancy to X-ray Shirley's lungs to double-check the positive blood identification. Shirley had started training as a nurse in Zimbabwe and recalled that she had received a TB booster. The doctor was confident that Shirley's positive TB identification could be attributed to her booster in earlier years. Finally, the "dangerous" time for X-rays for our unborn Timothy passed, and Shirley and unborn Timothy were able to be safely X-rayed. The results were negative for TB. We were elated. *"Like cold water to a thirsty soul, so is good news from a far country"* (Proverbs 25:25, ESV). We had come from a far country, and the TB update was indeed good news.

A few weeks later, we again received a letter from the immigration authorities. This time they requested that we appear in person before the immigration authorities in Minnesota. Shirley and I had no idea whether the summons was to welcome us or extradite us. It was now late in the eleventh hour, and we were believing against all odds that God would open doors. Regardless, we traveled back to St. Paul-Minneapolis, Minnesota, and met with immigration officials. This was our third attempt at gaining residency status and our third trip to St. Paul-Minneapolis.

We were warmly greeted. The interview was pleasant and quite brief. The immigration officials extended hearty congratulations and granted us our petition for residency. God had yet again gone before us and parted the Red Sea. *"Moses answered the people, 'Do not be afraid. Stand firm and you will see the deliverance the Lord will bring you today. The Egyptians you see today you will never see again. The Lord will fight for you; you need only to be still'"* (Exodus 14:13–14, NIV).

Abeka Curriculum

Teaching at the church school, Victory Academy, was a fun, learning and stressful experience all rolled up in one. The students used conservative Christian Abeka texts and workbooks and were on different lessons. I was their new teacher and attempted to have them all "catch up" so that students in each grade level would be working on the same lesson. I explained this to the students, telling them to "catch up" on their missing work for homework. The next day one student's mother wanted to know what I meant by "ketchup." Apparently she understood this to be a tomato sauce commonly associated with French fries and other foods. I realized my error and sought to correct it. It seemed my British Colonial African accent was too much for some.

The Abeka curriculum was the standard of excellence in Christian curricula. However, I had been trained in the latest British techniques, which included more experiential learning and critical thinking in a hands-on interdisciplinary classroom setting. We did lots of field trips and made learning relevant to students. The Abeka (and many other Christian curricula) I found were based on the biblical philosophy of "line upon line, precept upon precept." The extremely detailed curricula were carefully scripted for every aspect of the lesson, leaving nothing to chance for a new or not-so-new teacher. I found it burdensome and tedious at first and difficult to navigate with a combination grade class. This traditional "pouring in" approach was superior to many of the public school "standards-driven" approaches that left teachers free to select their accompanying texts and materials. Teachers at different public schools often used different texts but still the same standards. The public school curriculum was not as content-driven as the Christian school, which translates into public school students not learning as much content as those in many Christian schools. Later, when I completed my master's degree in school administration, I was able to reflect on the approaches to teaching in the New Testament and compare them with the Abeka approach. I found that there was a "perfect" balance of "pouring in" (Christian curricula) approaches and "drawing out" (public school approaches). The approach depended on the age of the audience and the subject matter at hand. Today I see value in the Christ-centered use of both approaches.

Blood Is Blue

One of the science lessons was on the circulatory system. I posed a question to my second- and third-grade class. "What color is blood inside your body?" Students immediately responded. About two-thirds said blood was blue inside your body, but upon exposure to air became red. About one-third said it was red. As a former instructor in the British Red Cross in Rhodesia (Zimbabwe), I was somewhat aghast and did everything I could to stop myself from guffawing. At lunch, I carefully posed the same question to a teacher friend. The teacher responded in kind, just as the majority of students had. Blood was blue inside your body but became red when exposed to air. How could such a brilliant mind have the wrong answer to this question? In subsequent years I have asked this question across several states and at every educational level. I have always received the same response and rationale. About two-thirds of respondents have claimed that blood is indeed blue inside the body but becomes red when exposed to air.

I made friends with Dr. Joe in our Sioux Falls church. We enjoyed playing racquetball together. I explained my predicament to Joe and asked if he had any ideas. His eyes twinkled as he said, "Yes, you."

"What?" I exclaimed. "What do you mean?"

"You can be the guinea pig," he explained. "I will draw blood from your arm into a syringe. There is no air in the syringe, and students will be able to observe the true color of blood inside your body." Joe smiled like a Cheshire cat.

I coordinated a whole school assembly so students could witness this "experiment." I was sure to ask students the leading question ahead of time and received the same responses from a show of hands.

I rolled up my arm. Joe swabbed the area with some antiseptic and a cotton ball, then ran a shiny needle into a protruding vein in my left arm. The vial quickly filled with crimson blood. Dr. Joe showed the vial to the students. He also explained that there was no air in the needle. One student called out, "That's African blood." Everyone laughed. But then an American teacher volunteered, and her blood was crimson, too. On a survey of hands in a "re-test," a hundred percent of students agreed that blood was red inside the human body. I asked one young girl who had been emphatic in my class that blood was blue inside your body, the same question. Her mother was a nurse. The student leaned forward, glaring bug-eyed, and puckered her lips. "At school it's red; at home it's blue." So that settled it. I have yet to discover the culprit for this erroneous and widespread belief about the color of blood inside the human body, but I have seen comments from the American Heart Association that talk about "bluish blood." Perhaps there are other explanations such as textbooks portraying arteries as red and veins as blue.

Levi

One recess I had an encounter of another kind with a second-grade student. In Zimbabwe, I had been the principal and teacher. Students generally listened well or faced firm consequences. In America, there was more tolerance for misbehavior, it seemed. It was cold outside, but we had recess outside up to minus 20° Fahrenheit. I had my light blue pants on and was freezing. Adjacent to the school was a vacant lot covered in snow interspersed with several patches of green grass. One of my second-grade students, Levi (not his real name), picked up a baseball and was about to throw it directly into another student's face right in front of him. I yelled loudly, "Levi!" He pivoted and glared. What followed was a tirade of expletives not fit for human consumption. I couldn't believe my ears. Students did not behave like this in Zimbabwe, at least not to teachers. Instinctively, I accelerated in Levi's direction. He turned and sped across the grassy snowy lot. I followed. The entire school stood gawking. I was gaining on Levi when he suddenly made a 90° turn in the middle of the lot. Unfortunately, I did not navigate the unexpected turn very well. I lost traction and slid into home base—except I was not playing baseball and there was no home base. A bright green band was painted along the entire outside seam of my light blue pant leg. I suddenly felt extremely humbled and ashamed. This was not the way to manage student behavior, regardless of what that student said. I resolved to "respond" and not "react" to any future misbehaviors. That resolve has kept me "cool and collected" over many years and many experiences. *Sorry, Levi!*

On another day, Levi ran away from school and led me and several other teachers on a wild goose chase for an hour or more. We finally caught up with him in the woods and delivered him to his mother. His mom was a wonderful lady and most gracious. It was difficult being a single parent. In time, and with lots of love and understanding, Levi's behavior improved. And so did mine!

Hands-on Integrated Teaching

The weather warmed up considerably over the next few months, and I decided to wear my light green Zimbabwe safari suit, which was a lightweight cotton top with long socks and short pants. Big mistake! The principal, Ms. H, called me into her office and sent me home to change. Embarrassing. I still had a lot to learn in this new culture.

I requested and gained permission to teach an integrated science unit, which mostly followed the Abeka curriculum but with fun activities. A small stream that ran through the property afforded immediate access to hands-on fun learning. The students studied the rate of flow of the stream, its average width and depth, and so on. They also collected samples of living and non-living things from in and around the shallow stream. One student found a harmless snake about fifteen inches long. With teacher guidance, a group of students set up a snake "fish" tank and began researching how to take care of the snake. The students were so excited about science. During one recess, a few students decided to go inside and clean out the tank. They had not asked permission. Unfortunately, the snake got loose, and the principal found out. Once the snake was recaptured, she promptly confiscated it and threw it outside. I was devastated. The snake was a pivotal part of our science lesson and kept students engaged in learning. I immediately stormed to the principal's office and asked if it was true that she had thrown out our snake. She firmly but gently confirmed that this was true and reminded me to monitor students better. Painful lesson learned.

Amazing Mother and Sons

Our two sons, Timothy James and Thomas Luke, were born in Sioux Falls, South Dakota. Both were seven pounds, five ounces, and twenty-one inches long. Both were born at the same hospital, in the same room, with the same bed number, and delivered naturally by the same stand-in delivery doctor—and by the same mother! Shirley's labor with Tim lasted six and a half hours and four and a half hours with Tom.

Tim was born on October 31, 1984. We call him our "hallelujah baby" because he was born on Halloween, which we do not celebrate due to its roots. Tom was born twenty months later on June 28, 1986. Both sons filled our lives with joy and made our family complete.

Artichokes and Weeds

We were in Sioux Falls for three summers. There was no school and therefore no income during the summer, so we were left to fend for ourselves. A former millionaire in the church offered me a job planting an experimental plot of Jerusalem artichokes at a congregant's farm. The job paid five dollars an hour in 1984. This was backbreaking work bending over and planting the bulbs. The days were hot with gnats flying up my nostrils. I worked with a Spanish church friend named Jamie, a married Bible college student who also needed income. We had some wonderful and uplifting conversations. The artichoke "investor" insisted that the artichoke's roots face magnetic north. I found this to be very strange but was confident he had researched the matter. Locating regular north was usually a challenge, but now I had to decipher magnetic north. However, I tried my best to honor his request—most of the time.

The artichokes grew quickly, and we had to pull the weeds to stop them from choking the leafy artichokes. Ironically, the weeds looked identical to the artichokes, except the underside of the artichokes' leaves was smooth, not furry. One day the investor boss stopped by to talk to Jamie and me. I was bent at a 90° angle pulling weeds and could not straighten up. It was strange how the investor boss did not seem to notice my unusual posture or facial agony. I could not walk for the next three days and had to crawl on my hands and knees. Most of my money went to a chiropractor. Amazingly, it was this chiropractor who gave me a copy of his booklet, titled *Learning Made Simple*.

I have shared this book over the years and used its Preview, Question, Read, Study, and Test (PQRST) principles. Years later, I developed "Dr. R.A.T.'s E-Z Reading to Learn Guide" based on similar principles, grounded in educational research. It asks, "What reading strategies does an efficient learner use *before*, *during* and *after* reading?" It then outlines practical strategies. Students from elementary grades to college level have benefited from this guide. Students in one college-level remediation class improved three years' worth in just two months of intensive reading remediation as measured by the exit assessment.

Kirby Salesman

The next summer I decided to try something a little less strenuous on my back. I saw an advertisement in the local paper for a Kirby vacuum cleaner salesman. I was excited about this novel adventure and aced the training. I soon learned that this was no "walk in the park." "Potential prospects" were lined up for us, but we had to purchase the promised "free gifts" that would be given to each client. Furthermore, some of the prospects (mainly little old ladies) lived fifty or more miles away and the gas was on me. This was high-pressure sales at its finest. If I failed to sell a Kirby, I didn't eat, plain and simple. I did a great job "teaching" and demonstrating the amazing Kirby attributes. In addition to powerful carpet cleaning, Kirbys came equipped with appendages that enabled one to unscrew lightbulbs, clean curtains, massage scalps and much more. I sold four Kirbys at a discount in the first week to personal friends who felt sorry for us, including one to our pastor, Neil. (Neil later returned his Kirby since he could not afford the payments.) After a month of horror stories trying to "extract the check from customers' back pockets to mine" (my Kirby trainer's instructions), I had still sold only four vacuum cleaners. I realized this was not paying the bills. In fact, it was quite the opposite. My Kirby trainer's words rang loudly in my ears: "You're as soft as a marshmallow, and you need to be as hard as a rock." Defrauding little old ladies was not my style. Perhaps I just didn't have the "sales" gene.

Factory Worker

I transitioned midsummer to a factory job I saw advertised in the local newspaper. The pay was minimal—$3.75 an hour—but at least the work was steady and the paycheck predictable. The workday started at 7:00 a.m. and ended at 3:30 p.m. We had half an hour for lunch. My first assignment was on a conveyor belt. The task was to use a crochet-like hook attached by a bicycle chain that ran over a cog wheel and was attached to a foot pedal. Depressing the foot pedal provided the main power needed to use the "crochet" hook extension and extend a spring in an aluminum window frame side channel. The trick was coordinating the left foot and right hand to stretch the spring and then wean it off over a rivet bar across the inside of the aluminum window tube, thus stretching the spring. Straightforward, right?

The lady opposite me did one of these spring stretching routines about every five seconds. She worked with mindless abandon and could converse simultaneously. She had apparently been doing this for years. My foot slipped off the metal pedal several times. It was hard to coordinate the leg and arm movements. The most difficult part was unhooking the spring from the crochet-type hook to slide over the rivet once the spring was stretched. Minutes went by, and I was becoming frustrated. Why wouldn't this thing work? My knuckles on my hand holding the bulky "crochet" hook kept scraping the thick rubber matting on the conveyor belt. At last, I did one. Yay! In the meantime, the aluminum U-shaped tubes kept coming slowly and steadily. I pushed them back when they came too close. Soon I had a small mountain of tubes. The lady opposite me was in hysterics. She told me to place the pile of tubes on the floor next to me. I did. Slowly, very slowly, I improved, and the kind lady opposite helped me to stay afloat by doing part of my share. I was deeply grateful. I nursed my bloodied knuckles and was glad when it was time to move to a different station.

One thing I could not understand was why everyone worked so quickly. I worked steadily. One day when the floor manager tapped me on the shoulder and said, "You do know that you have six weeks to reach quota speed?" I smiled sheepishly. Okay, now I knew. You produced or you were fired. I picked up the pace as best I could and started producing more. When the buzzer went off, signaling the end of the workday, it seemed like a marathon was underway as practically everyone ran for the exit. It was apparent that most workers couldn't wait for the day to be over.

I learned several life lessons here. First, Americans work hard and produce, otherwise they are fired. Second, if the pace is too fast (as in the conveyor belt), just push the load back or remove it temporarily, then when you have picked up the pace, complete the assignment. (Of course, a friendly coworker may assist, but not all the time.) Third, I needed to heed Ecclesiastes 9:10 better: "*Whatever your hand finds to do, do it with your might...*" (NKJV). These same sentiments are echoed in Colossians 3:17 and 23: "*And whatever you do in word or deed, do all in the name of the Lord Jesus, giving thanks to God the Father through Him. ... And whatever you do, do it heartily, as to the Lord and not to men*" (NKJV). My mama's words rang in my ears with the popular 1960s song by Ned Miller, "Do What You Do, Do Well." I have taken this song and the scriptures to heart and see their principles embodied in our two amazing sons. *So proud of you, Tim and Tom!*

We survived the second summer, but only by the grace of God. Neil had paid for our vehicle and the first ten months' rent for our home. Our income had almost doubled to about $8,000 a year, thanks partly to Shirley's working in the preschool three days a week. The poverty level in South Dakota at the time was $13,000. We did not complain. We had stepped out by faith from Africa and were following God. We knew the first few years would be hard. And they were. Whenever we stopped at a restaurant with a group of church folk after a Bible study, we would opt for a glass of water while others feasted and drank sodas. These were hard times, but we were thankful for God's blessings.

Shirley had written to her parents in Africa explaining what we were doing. Her dad wrote back and told us to "stop living like peasants." Clearly he did not understand that God had called us to follow Him. "*Better is one day in your courts than a thousand elsewhere; I would rather be a doorkeeper in the house of my God than dwell in the tents of the wicked*" (Psalm 84:10, NIV)

Telephone Company

I was "promoted" (by the Lord) in the third summer to a job in an indoor, air-conditioned facility at a telephone company. I met the owners through playing racquetball. Shirley had surprised me with a Christmas gift membership to a fitness center that had racquetball courts. I had already gleaned some experience playing with Dr. Joe and found that I could adapt my squash skills quite readily—once I realized I was playing with a much shorter racket and that the ball bounced differently. I saw two competitive players and asked if I could join them. They motioned that they would finish their game. It seemed like a game that lasted forever and that they had forgotten me, but eventually they beckoned me onto the court somewhat reluctantly. After a few games, however, they saw that I was quite skilled and asked if I would be able to play with them at other times. I did.

The phone company owners were used to winning, and my competitive nature made this harder. This resulted in court temper tantrums, a tirade of expletives, and them purposefully smashing their rackets into the wall. I knew this had to stop but enjoyed playing racquetball. One day, the vice-president of the company was on a trip, which left me playing with the president. After an eruption of pent-up frustration at not winning and the usual verbal outbursts, I told the president I would not be able to play with him again. I told him I was a Christian and did not want to be responsible for him on Judgment Day. He wasn't happy, and we parted ways.

Two weeks later I received a phone call from the president asking if I would come back and play racquetball. I paused momentarily then said, "Yes, sure. I'd love to." If he could humble himself to ask me to reconsider, I could do likewise and agree to play again. The court atmosphere changed noticeably. They started copying my lead in praising others for their good attempts. On rare occasions an expletive slipped out, but overall, there was a 175° turn. It was at this point that I asked them if they knew of a summer position. I explained that I was planning to go to Oral Roberts University to complete my master's degree in Christian School Administration. They told me they would get back with me. They did, a few days later. They created a position for me that was contingent upon my playing racquetball with them twice a week. Deal? Deal! *"Look at the birds of the air, for they neither sow nor reap nor gather into barns; yet your heavenly Father feeds them. Are you not of more value than they?"* (Matthew 6:26, NKJV).

Oral Roberts University

During our first year in America (1984), the principal of our Christian school had arranged a "field trip" to Oral Roberts University, a 700-mile trip south to Tulsa, Oklahoma. I had never heard of Oral Roberts University but quickly became acquainted with it. I was mesmerized by all the unique heavenly-like architecture and gigantic praying hands and prayer tower. I soon discovered that they offered a master's degree in

Christian School Administration. I knew there was no way "in the natural" that we could afford for me to go to ORU, plus I would have to have my Zimbabwe teaching credentials ratified as equivalent to an American bachelor's degree in education. However, the seeds were planted, and they grew.

I applied to have my credentials ratified through an international agency in Delaware. Eventually I was given the green light. Then, by faith, I applied to ORU. I had no idea whether I would be accepted or whether I would be able to perform at this level academically. I had worked very hard through school and saw myself as having to overperform just to achieve average results. As part of my application, I had to take the GRE (Graduate Record Examination). I was quite nervous about this, as it may confirm my deepest insecurities about lacking academic competence. The exam was heavy in math, reading comprehension and problem-solving. Everything was timed. Pressure!

I did my homework and several practice exams and felt I was as prepared as I could be. My results were marginal but opened up a way for acceptance at ORU where I started by correspondence halfway through the second year. I found the courses to be relatively easy after the demanding British system and achieved straight As. (This built my confidence, and I continued to achieve at this level through to the doctoral level years later.) I was a 4.0 GPA student all the way. *Thank You, Jesus!*

Rejection

The church in Sioux Falls, South Dakota, was joined by another pastor from Africa, who had been Neil's "spiritual" father. Neil invited him to co-lead the church. The transition was turbulent. Simon (not his real name), the new pastor, "uncovered" an "indiscretion" of Neil's and disciplined him by standing him down from ministry. Things were a mess. I thought I would be given the position first offered by Neil once the founding headmistress moved on. After all, Simon had often said that I should have been given the position. However, in a public statement to the church, Simon said there was no one "qualified" to take the position. I knew then that our time was up in Sioux Falls, South Dakota. I felt deeply rejected and overlooked.

This was a paralyzing blow to our future. We felt abandoned and adrift in a strange country with which we were slowly becoming acquainted. What now? My summer job was coming to an end. The present school job had no future. There was no way for us to go back to Africa. We were divinely stuck—another Exodus 14 moment. We couldn't go backward; we couldn't go forward. We were trusting God's plan for our lives. "'For I know the plans I have for you,' declares the Lord, 'plans to prosper you and not to harm you, plans to give you hope and a future'" (Jeremiah 29:11, NIV).

I was in the middle of wrapping up one ORU correspondence course titled "Holy Spirit in the Now." I came face to face with God in this course. Through the simple but powerful testimonies of God's provision as told by Oral Roberts and the reminder of God's promises in His Word, I had the divine revelation that God *alone* is my source. *God is my source.* My job was not my source. The church was not my source. God alone was and is my source. I looked upward. A load lifted from my shoulders. God would make a way. He always had. "'If you can'? said Jesus. 'Everything is possible for one who believes'" (Mark 9:23, NIV). "*Truly I tell you, if anyone says to this mountain, 'Go, throw yourself into the sea,' and does not doubt in their heart but believes that what they say will happen, it will be done for them. Therefore I tell you, whatever you ask for in prayer, believe that you have received it, and it will be yours*" (Mark 11:23–24, NIV).

During this period, we heard of the "Happy Hunters," Charles and Frances Hunter, an older couple who held healing services. They were down-to-earth and engaging. They did not put God in a box. If one prayer type didn't work, they would wait on the Lord and then try praying differently. It was clear that God was using them, especially in growing out people's limbs. I had never heard of God as the "Divine Physician and Chiropractor." People were healed and filled with God's Spirit. I wanted to learn more about this. Perhaps we'd learn more at Oral Roberts University, where Oral Roberts had been healed as a teen and then called to lead a healing ministry.

Once we saw the "writing on the wall" with Simon and the Christian school in Sioux Falls, I applied to ORU full-time. I had no idea where the funds would come from, but I said to God, "If You will meet me halfway,

I will have faith for the other half." I meant it. Shirley was particularly shy about incurring any debt. I agreed. It was God or bust.

Hitch Up Your Chariot

Then, just three weeks before ORU classes were to begin, a letter came from the ORU Registrar's office. Hooray! I qualified for a small grant just past the halfway amount. I called Shirley, who was visiting Noline. She listened and agreed. Then God spoke to me in my devotional time one morning through a line in 1 Kings 18:44: "*Hitch up your chariot and go down before the rain stops you*" (NIV). I took this quite literally. How would we hitch up our chariot, our Grand LeMans? And where would the funds come from?

We started packing for ORU on Monday and planned to leave at the end of the week. The only problem was that we had no idea how we were going to travel down to ORU with our stuff or where the money would come from. But God's Word had been clear: "*Hitch up your chariot.*"

While returning from a friend's apartment after work at the phone company, I passed a wooden slatted trailer for sale. I stopped and spoke to the owner. He was so proud of his trailer, which was built with trailer house springs. It was a six-foot by ten-foot open slat trailer, ideal for moving stuff—and we had accumulated some stuff in our two years and eight months in Sioux Falls. The owner wanted $500. I offered him $400, even though we did not have it. He told me "no," but also to come back the next day. The next day I went to work at the phone company, and the president asked what I was doing the rest of the week. I told him our plan was to travel to ORU on Friday. He told me to take the rest of the week off so we could pack up, and he paid me upfront for the entire week and said I did not have to return. I was elated. I immediately drove to where the trailer was—still for sale. The owner was pleasantly surprised when I produced the cash, especially after telling him I did not have the cash the previous day. He accepted $400. How great is our God! "*This is the confidence we have in approaching God: that if we ask anything according to his will, he hears us. And if we know that he hears us—whatever we ask— we know that we have what we asked of him*" (1 John 5:14–15, NIV).

A friend in the church welded a trailer mounting to the Grand Le-Mans, and I bought a trailer hitch. All I had to do was "hitch up my chariot" and load up the trailer.

Neil allowed us to store one trailer load of items in his basement. The remaining "stuff"—including lots of baby stuff for our two sons, Tim, twenty-two months old, and Tom, six weeks old—was packed in our trailer. In retrospect, we lacked wisdom in packing the trailer. I could not fit my big toe under the trailer hitch winch when it was fully wound. Usually the hitch would be several inches from the ground. The trailer was front-heavy and leaning forward like a seesaw. The rear of the tank-like Grand LeMans pointed downward. The 700-mile trip ahead of us was going to be a faith journey.

On the Thursday before we planned on leaving, Simon called us into his office. By this time Neil had been reinstated after being stepped down from the ministry for a year. God had given me a vivid dream about the need to reinstate Neil. I shared this with Simon, and he listened. Simon and the elders had decided to sponsor us $150 per month during our one year full-time at ORU. *Thank you, Simon.* God had answered prayer! The Red Sea was parting as we took steps of faith toward ORU. All praise and glory were due to God. *"Behold, I am doing a new thing; now it springs forth, do you not perceive it? I will make a way in the wilderness and rivers in the desert"* (Isaiah 43:19, ESV).

We departed for Tulsa on Friday. It was a very hot day. The trailer pushed and pulled our chariot LeMans down the interstate. A few hours into the drive, the air conditioning quit. Later, going up the lengthy Kansas inclines, I noticed large plumes of blue smoke billowing from the back of the Grand LeMans. What was that? We eventually found a cheap hotel in Wichita, Kansas, and bedded down.

The next morning, we continued our journey. Temperatures more than 100° Fahrenheit blew in through the open windows. Tom, our youngest son, was beet red. We were seriously concerned about heat-stroke and did everything we could to keep our sons cool. Finally, we reached ORU by late afternoon and stopped at the head of a very steep dip. ORU graduate housing lay on the other side. Cars would disappear in the dip for several seconds before reappearing on the other side. I was wondering how we were going to do this when I noticed a tall African American basketball player walking our way. I explained the predicament with the hitch and asked if he would stand on the back of the trailer to help raise the hitch. He willingly obliged. Then I floored the LeMans and several seconds later reappeared on the other side of the dip. The basketball player was hanging on for dear life. He appeared ashen and shaken. He had not expected to put his life on the line. *Sorry, ORU man!*

We unpacked in over 100° weather and then later that day moved again to a "safer" apartment on the backside of the apartment complex that had grass and a fence instead of a busy parking lot. The heat was record-breaking for Tulsa. We were exhausted but filled with joy—mission accomplished. Hallelujah! We made it to ORU. *Thank You, Jesus!* "*Hope deferred makes the heart sick, but a longing fulfilled is a tree of life*" (Proverbs 13:12, NIV). "*Delight yourself also in the Lord, and He shall give you the desires of your heart*" (Psalm 37:4, NKJV).

We'd braved multiple trials, and with the Lord's help, we were learning to fly *above the storms*. Everything was new. When we peeked ahead, thunderstorms were on the horizon, and so was an intense downdraft....

Shirley's Reflections

Life in America was challenging. Martin took the car to work, so I was alone during the day. Our neighbors on one side seemed to hibernate during winter. The neighbors on the other side could not speak English. When I found out I was pregnant, I made a list of things I needed. Shopping from that list reduced me to tears, as no one could understand me. The following are examples of how British English and American English differ:

English cot – American crib (An American cot is what we call a stretcher.)
English pram – American buggy
English pushchair – American stroller
English dummy – American pacifier
English nappies – American diapers

There were so many different words that I thought I was a total alien.

I was also rather embarrassed when it came to doing my laundry. There was a laundromat about four blocks away. I would drag my laundry in a suitcase on wheels, often slipping on the icy pathway. It was bitterly cold. One day, the sun was shining brightly, so I hung my laundry out to dry. Many hours later, when I went to bring it in, I found that the clothes had frozen solid. How embarrassing! It was below -30° Fahrenheit. (-34.44° Celsius). I had been totally deceived by the sun. I often wonder what the neighbors thought that day.

CHAPTER 8

Miracle Year

(1986-1987)

Crisis Faced: Provision – Basic Needs
Crisis: Financial – College and Living
Storm: Microburst – Can Cause Extensive Surface Damage

Doctor Dream on the Altar

Our year at ORU was a lifesaver. We were temporarily out of the malaise of church politics and unmet expectations and immersed in our ORU life. Shirley stayed home in the apartment and nurtured our two growing sons. She also typed my papers on a typewriter, plus papers for our ORU friend Jim. Timothy was twenty-two months old and growing tall, and Thomas was just six weeks old. My day started at 6:00 a.m. After my devotional time and breakfast, I rode my yellow bicycle about a mile to the ORU campus. I was diligent in my studies and spent most of my time in the main library when not in classes. I had loaded up with nineteen graduate credit hours for the first semester so that I could graduate in May of 1987. I had already completed one year's studies at ORU by correspondence in Sioux Falls. The semester was challenging but exciting. I wanted to learn as much as I could about Christian School Administration.

The lady opposite our upstairs apartment had ten kids. She was a medical student going through the "free" ORU medical school that required graduating doctors to pay back in time served on the mission field. Meeting this lady stirred up a latent desire to be a medical doctor. I had dropped advanced chemistry in my last year of high school in Rhodesia (Zimbabwe), and with it also my chance at entering medical school at the University of Rhodesia. Four years later while completing my Bachelor of Education degree at the University of Rhodesia (now Zimbabwe), I met a medical student who practiced Shotokan karate at the same dojo where I trained (and later became the instructor). I investigated the possibilities of medical school but soon realized that I risked not completing my bachelor's degree or scoring sufficiently high enough to enter medical school. I decided to put my deeply held aspiration on hold for another three years to see how I adjusted to teaching. In the meanwhile, I married Shirley, emigrated to America and enrolled in the Christian School Administration program at ORU.

I again dived deeply into the possibility of pursuing my dream to become a medical doctor. I spoke to people, researched the matter and counted the cost. I was excited about the possibility of pursuing this direction at last. However, the daunting cost of another thirteen years of my life dedicated to studies and medical missions was too high a cost for my family. I realized that Tim would be fifteen and Tom thirteen by the time I would be free from medical missions' obligations. I could see them growing up without my active leadership in their lives. I didn't want that. They were way too precious a gift from God for me to pursue my own dreams at their expense—to say nothing about Shirley. Furthermore, I really did love education and school administration and felt that I excelled in these areas. The main factor in deciding not to pursue medicine at ORU was the lack of internal peace. Every time I pursued the medicine option, peace was elusive. When I did not actively pursue it, peace returned and flooded my soul. I finally recognized the pattern. No peace. Peace. No peace. Peace. I decided to put my dream of becoming a medical doctor once and for all on God's altar and trust Him completely with our future. Peace.

Christmas Miracles

Christmas 1986 approached with the certainty of a rolling freight train. We felt alone on the earth, adrift from the church we had come to from

Africa. It was as though we were caught in a strong downward vortex that threatened to suck life from us. The vision we had stepped out to fulfill—full-time ministry with Neil, our friend and pastor in Sioux Falls, South Dakota—had evaporated, but God in His mercy had made a way for full-time attendance at ORU. We attended Billy Joe Daugherty's church and were part of a vibrant home group attached to the church. Our involvement in ORU and church was a saving grace for us. Slowly we began to surface, free from the powerful vortex of leaden disappointment that had been sucking us ever downward. Slowly we began to see the light of day. Sharon Daugherty's songs and those of David Ingles on the radio were especially encouraging and helped to rebuild our confidence. Then the week before Christmas, something happened.

We were at church and Pastor Billy Joe (himself a former student of ORU) challenged us to "sow a seed out of our need." We had ten dollars left for the month and no means of earning or gaining additional funds. We had no money for Christmas and no funds for the next semester. I felt like Nehemiah rebuilding the walls of Jerusalem. I was halfway through the school year, but the road ahead seemed like a dead end. Still, we responded to the call to sow seed by sowing all we had. That was Sunday. We understood a little about how the widow in Mark 12:41–44 may have felt: "*Now Jesus sat opposite the treasury and saw how the people put money into the treasury. And many who were rich put in much. Then one poor widow came and threw in two mites, which make a quadrans. So He called His disciples to Himself and said to them, 'Assuredly, I say to you that this poor widow has put in more than all those who have given to the treasury'*" (Mark 12:41–43, NKJV).

On Monday, I approached one of my professors and shared the predicament for the upcoming semester. I had already signed up for the maximum class load to finish the degree by May of 1987. I spent practically all my time working on ORU studies except for family and church time and exercise. I also enjoyed taking Tim and Tom for rides on the back of my yellow bicycle. On Fridays we would go to McDonald's to buy French fries as a little treat for Tim. Tom was not yet on solid foods. There was no additional time to work to earn money to pay for school. If I did work, I would have to drop some classes and extend the school year, then continue to work to pay for the school year and ORU lodging.

Our financial situation seemed to be quickly spinning out of control, or at least out of *our* control.

On Tuesday, Jim, my ORU friend, came to dinner and left a gift of shoes for Timothy. He must have been intuitive to this need as Tim needed new shoes. On Wednesday, a couple knocked on our door and said they had been asked to deliver a box of Christmas goodies, including a turkey with all the trimmings. The following day, we opened our apartment door to discover a huge box replete with all the trimmings for a Christmas dinner, chocolates, pecan pie (which was new to us), and colorfully wrapped gifts for each of us. We were deeply touched. God was taking care of us. Later that day, the last day of the fall semester, the professor I'd spoken to called me to his office and directed me to the Registrar's office. He never explained why. When I arrived at the Registrar's office, the lady told me to sign some forms. I was awarded a little-known scholarship retroactively to be part of the semester we were ending and proactively for the upcoming term. Hallelujah! God's faithfulness was being manifested. I could continue to attend ORU full-time without having to reduce my course load and look for a job. *Thank You, Jesus!* On Friday, our good friends Ann and Jeff drove down from Sioux Falls, South Dakota, to stay with us for Christmas. They brought Christmas gifts and more Christmas food, including a turkey. God had undertaken beyond anything we could have thought of or imagined. We were able to share some of these abundant blessings with a neighbor (the one with ten children). The God of "immeasurably more" had come to our rescue yet again. "*Now to Him who is able to do exceedingly abundantly above all that we ask or think, according to the power that works in us*" (Ephesians 3:20, NKJV).

Stitches

I was holding Tim's hand as we walked down a road in the graduate residences. Timothy was active and jumping. His hand slipped out of mine, and he fell backward, splitting his head open. I felt terrible. Stitches were needed. There were a few other times when I was the cause of my son having accidents. On one occasion later in our Michigan apartment, I was playing ball with Tim. He was in front of the basement apartment window "box" and fell back trying to catch a ball

I had thrown. More stitches. On another occasion when we were in South Carolina, I was up in a tree working on a project and asked five-year-old Timothy to throw up a saw. I was supposed to catch the saw by the handle, but it slipped through my fingers. The handle caught his eyebrow. Stitches again. *Sorry, Timothy. You were so trusting. I have always tried to protect you.*

Restoration Dream

I had a vivid dream one night about the "Iron Lady" school principal, Ms. H, at the Sioux Falls, South Dakota, Christian school. She was the principal who "made" me follow the rigid Abeka curriculum and who had thrown my classroom snake away. She was also the person who introduced me to ORU when on a school staff field trip. In the dream, I could see Ms. H weeping. I sensed that she cared deeply about her faculty and all her students. It was just that I was not used to being placed in a "straitjacket," curriculum-wise, when teaching. I could see that my attitude was wrong. Instead of resisting the leadership, I should have embraced it. I awoke from my dream and drafted a handwritten letter. I asked Ms. H to forgive me for my resistance and wrong attitude.

When Ms. H received the letter, she woke up her husband from his nap and read it to him. They both wept. She sent me the most beautiful letter and a little gift for the family. *"But I say to you that whoever is angry with his brother without a cause shall be in danger of the judgment. And whoever says to his brother, 'Raca!' shall be in danger of the council. But whoever says, 'You fool!' shall be in danger of hell fire. Therefore if you bring your gift to the altar, and there remember that your brother has something against you, leave your gift there before the altar, and go your way. First be reconciled to your brother, and then come and offer your gift"* (Matthew 3:22–24, NKJV).

Healing

Our son Thomas experienced a miraculous healing while we were at ORU. At only a few months old, he developed a lump on his navel. One Sunday morning, guest speaker Marilyn Hickey had a word of knowledge for those with lumps in their bodies to come forward for prayer. Shirley took Tom up for prayer and then immediately checked him, but the lump was still there. However, the lump had completely disappeared by the time we arrived back at our upstairs apartment. *All glory to God our Healer.*

Hard Work

ORU was a confidence builder for me. I had struggled somewhat academically at school under the streamlined British educational system in Rhodesia (Zimbabwe). This made me feel less than adequate. However, I was a hard worker and used setbacks as opportunities to improve academically. Once at college in Bulawayo, Rhodesia (Zimbabwe), I noticed that I had some of the highest grades among my peers. The grades qualified me for acceptance at the University of Rhodesia to finish up my B.Ed. degree where I continued to earn good grades for the most part. At ORU I earned a 4.0 (which is straight As) in the master's degree and maintained this GPA later in the doctoral program. I give all glory to God as He honored my persistence and diligence. I continue to be an overachiever to this day, doing "my utmost for His highest" (like the title of the book by Oswald Chambers).

Job Hunting

The end of the year approached rapidly. Soon I would be graduating. God graciously supplied a mechanic who repaired our ailing transmission in the Grand LeMans. In the meanwhile, I began making inquiries about schools that were looking for principals and filling out copious applications. This was a learning process. I interviewed locally at a Christian school in Tulsa and remember being asked what my five-year plan was. Seriously? We were walking by faith and trusting God for the *next meal.* I had not considered a five-year plan.

In retrospect, and after many years of training in educational leadership, I completely see the value in planning proactively, but in April 1987, my five-year plan was nonexistent. I think the interviewing board was not impressed with my response when I said it was the same as Abraham's. *"By faith Abraham, when called to go to a place he would later receive as his inheritance, obeyed and went, even though **he did not know where he was going**"* (Hebrews 11:8, NIV, emphasis added).

Two additional schools expressed interest in interviewing me. One was a sizeable K-12 Christian school in downtown Philadelphia. The other was a small K-8 country Christian school near Grand Rapids, Michigan. We managed, with God's enabling, to purchase round-trip air tickets for the four of us. By this time, Tim was three and three-quarters years old, and Tom was just over a year. We had used all our money on air tickets but were promised reimbursement by the Philadelphia school. We arrived on Friday afternoon. The reimbursement surfaced on Sunday afternoon, but not without a gentle but persistent reminder from Shirley as we desperately needed diapers for our sons.

The Philadelphia school was surrounded by a high block wall with barbed wire on top. The gates were wrought iron and locked. We were escorted around the school and told that the local Mafia sent their children to the school. They were looking for a strong leader. After the school tour, we were invited to join the pastor and his wife for a family lunch on Sunday, Mother's Day. Since the "adult" table was full, they asked us to sit with the children. We found this to be rather dishonoring and wondered what else might be in store, should I be offered this position and accept it.

From Philadelphia, we flew to Grand Rapids, Michigan, where I interviewed at a small K-8 Christian school in a nearby town. The board chairman was the head of a local telephone company and was most welcoming. We accepted the position, and the board graciously offered to move us from Tulsa.

Cross-Country Move

Nick and Dwaine (not their real names), school board members at the Christian school near Grand Rapids, Michigan, drove the almost 900 miles one-way to Tulsa in Oklahoma. They helped us load our trailer, then pulled it to Michigan with Dwaine's truck. They offloaded then turned around with the trailer and picked up the remainder of our belongings we had left with our pastor friends in Sioux Falls, South Dakota. This journey was about 750 miles one way. All told, they traveled over 3,300 miles—and did not charge us a dime. We felt blessed and believed that we were (literally) moving in the right direction—God's direction. *Thank you, Nick and Dwaine, for demonstrating the love of God to us.* "So *he answered and said, "'You shall love the Lord your God with all your heart, with all your soul, with all your strength, and with all your mind,"* and *"your neighbor as yourself"'"* (Luke 10:27, NKJV).

En route to nearby Grand Rapids, Michigan, from ORU in Tulsa, Oklahoma, we detoured to Sioux Falls, South Dakota, and checked in with Neil and Noline, our former pastor and his wife. We also attended Ann and Jeff's wedding (the friends who had visited us at Christmas). While visiting, we attended another healing outreach conducted by the Happy Hunters. We watched extensive healing training video materials and worked through the accompanying training manual. Immediately we started to implement what we had been learning.

We prayed for one elderly lady friend named Norma. She had severe upper back pain. She was instantly healed and gave glory to God. *"…I am the Lord, who heals you"* (Exodus 15:26, NIV).

A few days later, we launched out on the next chapter of our lives and drove from Sioux Falls, South Dakota, to a small town near Grand Rapids, Michigan, our "new" home.

God had miraculously provided and helped us *soar above the storms* of financial need and provision. Around the corner, cold air masses were colliding with warm air….

Shirley's Reflections

Oral Roberts University was a healing balm for us. Although we had very little money, our faith was stretched, and it was exciting to see how God repeatedly met our needs. *"Now to him who is able to do immeasurably more than all we ask or imagine, according to his power that is at work within us"* (Ephesians 3:20, NIV). We were totally refreshed and ready for the new assignment in Michigan.

CHAPTER 9

Michigan

(1987-1990)

Crisis Faced: Estrangement – Broken Promises
Crisis: Midlife – Emotional Turbulence
Storm: Blizzard – Severe Snowstorm, Strong Winds, Low Visibility

Year One
Principal
The school year launched into action like a racehorse in the Kentucky Derby. I was the principal of a K-8 independent Charismatic church school and taught the upper grades. There was a buzz in the church and school with all the activity. In addition to leading the school and teaching, I served as the custodian when needed and helped in public relations.

My main role in public relations was to recruit students. This paid dividends when another small struggling Christian school decided to join forces with us. Recruiting students was an ongoing and time-consuming endeavor. Board meetings and preparation for them were other responsibilities. Still, I was happy to be serving in a Christian school ministry.

Shirley had recovered from her first-ever major sinusitis attack that had her bedridden and throwing up. She even stopped breastfeeding our youngest son, Tom. She gradually recovered with the loving care of Judy, a school board member's wife.

Shirley acquired her babysitting license and before long was "babysitting" eleven children under five years of age (including Tom and Tom). Her day started with the first two children arriving at 5:30 a.m. She did double-shift breakfasts and lunches and gave one student dinner. She also put the children on and off the school bus. During the day she taught the Abeka curriculum to the little ones. Shirley's babysitting was more of a combination of preschool and daycare. By 8:30 p.m. when the last child left, she was thoroughly exhausted.

Our income increased from $4,500 in our first year in America to $20,000 in our fourth year. We were grateful for the increase and continued to tithe. When Christmas came that first year, the school board chairman along with his wife came around to our apartment with a box of gifts for the family paid for out of their own pocket. Their generosity was deeply appreciated, especially considering our lean financial situation.

Healing Anointing

We had been in Michigan for a few months and the teaching from the Happy Hunters who had visited Sioux Falls, South Dakota, was still fresh in my mind and heart. I so enjoyed the simplicity and authenticity of their healing ministry. One of the areas God used them was in growing out limbs. I had never heard of this, but it was evident that the Holy Spirit was at work healing people's bodies, emotions and minds through this powerful ministry.

While sitting downstairs in our kitchen one evening enjoying a home-cooked meal by my beloved Shirley, I had my arms dangling lazily at my side at the kitchen table. I became curiously aware of a phenomenon that I have to this day. My right arm started *growing* toward the floor, and I kept pulling it upward, much like a slinky. I could sense the presence of the Holy Spirit so strongly. Later, upstairs, I did what I saw the Hunters do and stretched my arms in front of me parallel to the floor. My arms started growing. First was the right arm, then it went back; then the left arm grew and went back—sometimes three or more inches. I was awed at the presence and power of

God. Later I noticed a sensation of honey dripping from the fingers of my right hand and a sensation of a light electrical current. Over the years, I have prayed for hundreds of people in similar Happy Hunter-style fashion, and I have seen Jesus do remarkable miracles, usually immediately. I have often sensed God's healing anointing. "... *To another gifts of healing by that one Spirit, ...then gifts of healing...*" (1 Corinthians 12:9, 28 NIV).

At one of our morning school chapels, I asked who needed healing prayer. I was surprised at how many K-8 students raised their hands to receive prayer. Those wanting prayer lined up by the piano. I asked each student what they wanted Jesus to do for them and laid hands on each one. Every student prayed for that morning was healed. I found that it was so easy to pray for children because of their child-like faith.

One girl from our apartment complex attended our church and needed prayer one Sunday. I prayed for the young girl, who then got up from the pew and ran around the church. She had come with a broken leg but left healed.

Shirley had a lump in her breast that she was concerned about. A visiting evangelist announced that there was someone there with a lump on her breast. He said that the individual should check herself in the restroom. Shirley's lump had completely disappeared. "*But to you who fear My name the Sun of Righteousness shall arise with healing in His wings; and you shall go out and grow fat like stall-fed calves*" (Malachi 4:2, NKJV). *Thank You, Jesus!*

Learning Curve

The first year was a learning curve and was my first headship in the United States. The stress of being a principal, combination class middle-school teacher, janitor and public relations spokesperson was internalized, and it manifested in massive gout explosions in my big toe joints. I could hardly walk. Soon it was June and summer, and a new board chairperson was installed.

Written into my first-year contract was permission to return to Zimbabwe for the summer. However, the "new" school board chair dropped a news bomb. "You cannot go back to Zimbabwe. You need to work at the school!" This was not what I had negotiated. Despite my protest and showing the new chair the contract, his mind was fixed. He had not been part of the original decision and believed the school needed my attention.

Shirley and I were in a dilemma—another rock and a hard place. We had been there before. We prayed. Somehow God would deliver us. We could stay in Michigan at the school and lose our air tickets and the opportunity to visit loved ones back in Zimbabwe, or we could go to Zimbabwe and lose my job in Michigan. After much prayer, we resolved to return to Zimbabwe and trust God with our future. After all, we were in His service.

Thankfully the pastor stepped in and "smoothed" things over. We were permitted to go to Africa without the risk of losing my job. *"I sought the Lord, and He heard me, and delivered me from all my fears"* (Psalm 34:4, NKJV).

Africa

Our trip back to Zimbabwe and family members was medicine to the soul. *"Hope deferred makes the heart sick, but a longlining fulfilled is a tree of life"* (Proverbs 13:12, NIV). We reconnected with Shirley's family in Bulawayo and borrowed the family Renault 4. Tim was almost four years old, and Tom was two.

Jane, Shirley's sister, and Ken, her brother-in-law, had traveled from Johannesburg, South Africa, to Shirley's parents in Bulawayo, Zimbabwe. Ken had to return to work after a couple of days but left his family in Bulawayo to further enjoy the long-awaited Sallabank reunion. We celebrated Christmas early before setting off for the Ratcliffe reunion in Mutare (in the eastern highlands on the other side of the country).

Somabula (Now Somabhula)

We traveled from Bulawayo and looped off the main Bulawayo-Harare Road to visit my childhood school in Somabula. I was excited to travel down the dusty lane to the old farmhouse—except the farmhouse had been demolished and another built nearby. Shirley could not understand what I saw in this isolated patch of African bush filled with blue gum trees, but memories flooded my soul.

I pointed to an old truck cab shell and told the boys stories of how the four Ratcliffe kids played imaginary road trips. I was the eldest at ten, then Mary at six and a half, Kiey (Brian) at four, and Liam at three. We often climbed the banks of the railway "balloon," an elliptical railroad structure set twenty-five feet up on mounded earth with railroad gravel and tracks atop. This allowed locomotives to travel around and change their direction. Dad worked a half a mile up the sandy road at a busy railroad juncture that redirected rail traffic to Bulawayo, Harare or Lorenço Marques (now Maputo) in neighboring Mozambique. It was an important juncture.

When Liam had turned four years of age, he was allowed to visit the local elementary school. Philda, a young energetic African maid who lived in a farm dwelling next to our home, worked for my parents. She would hoist Liam onto her back and carry him the mile or so to the Somabula Primary School while Mary, Kiey and I tagged along.

Somabula Primary was filled with so many memories. It was a small school of just twenty-one K-6 students. It seemed that "new kids" were bullied, especially if they were different. As the son of "Irish" parents, I was different and endured some bullying from other students. However, I proved myself as the goalkeeper of the soccer team, and over time we became friends. Our tiny school beat the much larger Cecil John Rhodes Primary School in Gwelo (now Gweru) twenty-one miles away, three goals to two. We were elated. Students from every level were needed to make up our soccer team. The situation was the same for other sports, including cricket.

I learned how to swim in Somabula. The headmaster and my teacher, Mr. R, apparently knew that I could swim in the shallow end but that I hadn't ventured into the deep end. One day I was standing by the edge of the deep end pondering the possibility of jumping in, when I felt a gentle but decisive nudge and "jumped" into the deep end. I surfaced and swam. Voila! I could now swim in the deep end!

Our classes were multiple-grade classes with only two teachers for the entire school. One day during a history lesson, I looked through the open door toward the nearby railroad track. A black crow on a nearby tree branch caught my attention. I was transfixed. "Look at the little bird, sir," I blurted out in the middle of the lesson. It became immediately apparent that this intrusion was not welcomed. Still, I was struck by the majesty and poise of the crow.

One day after school, classmates and I discovered boxing gloves in the all-purpose room in a nearby building. I had previously boxed for a little while in Bulawayo when my parents had returned to Rhodesia after an earlier hiatus to England during native uprisings in the early 1960s. I was to take part in a regional boxing tournament, but my mother feared that I would be knocked out, and my boxing career was abruptly terminated at the age of eight. But now I was ten going on eleven years of age. The excitement of boxing with classmates was too much to resist. A couple of us donned gloves and "went at it"—for fun, of course. And that is when our "fun" was abruptly interrupted by the headmaster. He told us we were not allowed to play with the "gloves." I hadn't known that there were "gloves" and knew of no such rule. Regardless, I was guilty. "Remind me on Monday," quipped Mr. R.

Monday came. My conscience was working overtime. Mr. R had said to "remind him," so I did. He did not say "what" to remind him of, so my almost eleven-year-old brain said, "Sir, you said to remind you." And that is when I received my first "dorking" (spanking). Ouch! Now I knew what he meant.

Mr. R was strict but fair. I was sorry to see him leave a few months later. His replacement was an "Irishman" with whom my parents connected.

However, my second "dorking" followed soon after his arrival. One Friday, the new headmaster noticed my messy handwriting. I was "dorked" (spanked). On Monday, my schoolbook was still on his desk, and he wanted to "dork" me again. I protested as he had already done so. Uncharacteristically, he relented.

After completing homework and usually on the weekends, I rode donkeys with an African teen friend in the compound next to our home. Sometimes I would go alone if my friend was not available. Typically I would mount "my" donkey and head off into the vast African bush with my Rhodesian Ridgeback-cross Alsatian (German Shepherd) dog Queenie. I loved Queenie. She had two eyebrow "eyes" above her normal eyes and would talk to me with her "eyes" by moving them up one side or the other and tilting her head. She knew how to get through to me.

Queenie would surge through the tall grass as I scurried along on the donkey riding bareback with only a short rope around the donkey's neck for control. We spent hours of fun riding the Somabula Flats (open prairie-like grasslands). Queenie would yelp and bark excitedly when she spotted a deer, then bound through the tall grass in pursuit. Sometimes she would chase rabbits. One day she chased a rabbit down a hole. I found a stick and poked down the hole, hoping to dislodge the rabbit so Queenie could continue the chase. Alas, fur filled the end of the stick, and the rabbit remained steadfast.

On another day, Queenie chased a rabbit into the round thatched "shed" on our property. She had it between her paws and stared it down. The rabbit was wide-eyed, staring helplessly at this predator. "Let go," I instructed Queenie. She looked at me with one of her four eyes as though to say, "Really? I want to play some more," but obediently backed up. The rabbit shot out of the building with Queenie in hot pursuit. She never caught the rabbit.

One afternoon a drunk African male neighbor was sauntering along the pathway outside our property line en route to the compound annexed to our yard. A wire "climb-through" fence marked our one-acre property. The man attracted Queenie's attention, and she started barking. The man picked up a rock and threw it at Queenie. I immediately came to Queenie's defense and hurled a rock at him. The rock struck him on the head. The sudden jolt to his skull arrested his attention, and he climbed through the fence wires. He bore down on me. Pain and rage filled his eyes. He climbed through the wire fence, stormed my way and grabbed me by the throat. Queenie circled behind him and attacked his rump with ferocity. He immediately relinquished his hold and swore.

"I will tell your fasser [father]," the man yelled in English in a thick African brogue. "I will tell your fasser."

"I don't care if you tell my fasser," I yelled back, imitating the African brogue. "I will tell my fasser what you did. He will come to you," I threatened back. In retrospect, I should have secured Queenie and avoided the incident and my colonial white imperial disrespect." *Sorry, sir.*

Memories continued to flood my mind. I remembered setting a bucket trap, carefully hidden and flush with ground level. A third of the bucket was filled with water, with a "mealie cob" (white maize cob) pierced through the center with a length of wire. The wire was secured to the bucket's handle on either side. The idea was that the mice, which were a menace to our chickens and their eggs, would come and nibble on the maize cob. The cob would spin under the weight of the mouse, hurling the mouse to its death in the water below. My record catch was twenty-one mice! So many memories, but soon it was time to move on from Somabula to our next destination.

Our next stop was a couple of hours down the road at Umniati (now Munyati). We passed by the country elementary school where I had first been principal and teacher and Shirley a teacher, then on to the club on top of the lone hill. We recounted memories of swimming and playing squash and of friendships with farmers and local village folk. We then stopped at a nearby farm belonging to Jay and Patsy. Patsy had been an amazing loyal school secretary when I was the principal. Patsy and farmer friends plus Shirley and I would play tennis at the local club on Saturday afternoons as Jay, Patsy's husband, watched while sipping a beverage.

We departed later in the afternoon and stayed with friends overnight in the capital city of Harare.

Farewell Again

The next morning we departed for Mutare (formerly Umtali), about a five-hour drive from Harare. We celebrated Christmas at my parents' home along with my siblings. A few days later we completed our family and friends' "tour" of Zimbabwe and headed *home* to Bulawayo. We passed over the giant Birchenough Bridge that spanned the Save River, made our way through Masvingo (formerly Fort Victoria, where I was raised in my teenage years), and then traveled on to Shabani (now Zvishavane), about sixty-plus miles away where I had started teaching. While visiting the little church Shirley and I had attended, we found out that Neil, our former pastor in Shabani, was vacationing from America and visiting friends in Mashaba, about halfway back to Masvingo, my hometown. We decided to double back and found Neil and his friends. We enjoyed an afternoon's barbeque, or "braaivleis," as we say in southern Africa. What were the chances of crisscrossing the globe and meeting up with our former pastor who had married us? "*The steps of a good man are ordered by the Lord*" (Psalm 37:23a, KJV). *Thank You, Jesus, for this divine encounter.* It refreshed our souls!

While in Bulawayo, I received a phone call from the school in Michigan explaining that the books had come in for the new school year and that they did not have the money to pay for both my salary and the books. They wanted to know what they should do. Of course, I told them to go ahead and pay for the books. Somehow God would take care of us as He always had. *"Even to your old age, I am He, and even to gray hairs I will carry you! I have made, and I will bear; even I will carry, and will deliver you"* (Isaiah 46:4, NKJV).

It was tempting to stay in Zimbabwe and serve in a Christian school where we might be appreciated. However, I still had several thousand dollars in loans to pay off in America and needed to return. Plus, God had called us to America. *"From the east I summon a bird of prey; from a far-off land, a man to fulfill my purpose. What I have said, that I will bring about; what I have planned, that I will do"* (Isaiah 46:11, NIV).

O'Hare Miracle

We caught a bus from Shirely's hometown of Bulawayo, in Zimbabwe, to Johannesburg, South Africa, and boarded an overnight flight from O.R. Tambo International Airport. Soon we were winging our way back to America via a connecting flight in London, England. We knew we had a tight shuttle connection across London to catch the next flight from Gatwick International Airport to JFK International Airport in New York. The flight attendant had agreed to usher us off the plane at the top of the line to help make the connection. We had a two-hour window.

We landed at Heathrow International Airport on time early the following morning. Tim (four) and Tom (two) were wide-eyed and full of adventure. Upon exiting the gate, we stopped and reached into a carry-on bag for a wrist "child leash" so that our energetic boys would not wander. Early morning throngs of people scuttled in droves in seemingly mindless abandon to their connecting flights at one of the world's busiest airports. In the "twinkling of an eye," Tom was nowhere to be seen. Tim was secured with his wrist leash, but Tom had suddenly disappeared. Vanished. Completely. *"Jesus,"* I cried out silently in desperation, breathing deeply. Panic tried to erupt like the explosive thrust of a NASA rocket launching into space. I controlled my breathing. Shirley and I quickly agreed on a plan. She would stay with Tim and keep looking around for Tom. I would scour the area.

I went with the flow of human traffic. A two-year-old could disappear very easily in such a mass of moving humanity—or be kidnapped. I could not let my mind go there. I prayed in the Spirit. Silently. My eyes were super focused. I was hypervigilant. I went as quickly and as methodically as I could through the hurried human masses of oblivion. By now I was praying out loud in the Spirit, which was drowned by the roar of human traffic. God's supernatural peace came over my mind and spirit. Then I heard the distinct voice of the Holy Spirit, "*Turn around and go the other way.*" This did not make sense since I had been "going with the flow" of human traffic. However, I immediately yielded, turned and pressed against the flow of traffic. My world slowed down and turned from color to black and white. I should have been panicked out of my mind. But I wasn't in my mind. I felt strangely surrounded by God's reassuring presence. "*Whether you turn to the right or to the left, your ears will hear a voice behind you, saying, 'This is the way; walk in it'*" (Isaiah 30:21, NIV).

And then I spotted him. Tom was only steps away from sliding glass doors that opened automatically onto the traffic-crazy busy London street with black taxi cabs and red double-decker busses roaring in both directions. I bolted over to Tom and grasped him with both hands and held him closely in my arms. He stared at me with childlike innocence. He was merely exploring his surroundings and was nonplussed. No big deal.

Just then, an English bobby (police officer) complete with an impeccably smart uniform and hard black "bobby" helmet, who was standing statue-like at the far side of the moving glass doors, quipped out loud so I could hear, "Some parents just don't know how to take care of their children." I breathed deeply and chose to ignore this careless comment. My natural inclination to rearrange his stoic visage was constrained. He had no idea what this father (and mother) had gone through in the last fifteen minutes. No idea!

When I reconnected with Shirley, I quickly found out her story. She had asked a couple near her, who were total strangers, if they could look after Tim and our carry-on bags while she connected with airport personnel to announce to be on the lookout for a missing child. It seemed like the right thing to do at the time, but in later moments, Shirley could not believe she had entrusted our son Tim to total strangers. *Thank You, Jesus, for Your divine protection over our children!*

We made it to the baggage carousel, very conscious of our tight connection. We had already "lost" precious minutes. We waited and waited. And waited. After what seemed like an eternity, our bags surfaced. Last. More deep breaths and prayers.

We found the Gatwick shuttle service, only to be told that the regular bus had broken down and that a replacement was being sent. By the time the replacement shuttle bus arrived, we barely had time to reach Gatwick before our departure flight to the United States. Still, we would try. Everything was in God's hands. We were exhausted from the flight and adrenaline-rushing events of the morning and settled into our seats for the transit ride across London to Gatwick International Airport, an hour or so away. Finally, we arrived at Gatwick—just as the boarding gates closed. Aaagh! We were deeply disappointed. We prayed. "Father, show us the way." It was clear that God had another plan for us. Our tickets (that theoretically could not be changed) were thankfully reissued for the next morning, and we were directed to an English country mansion "bed and breakfast" several miles away set on several hectares. The boys were excited to see the horses when we arrived. We settled in and enjoyed an evening meal. Soon we were fast asleep in our plush beds.

The overnight break at the B & B was welcomed. Our spirits and bodies were revitalized, and we enjoyed a traditional English breakfast with sausage, bacon, eggs and baked beans before being shuttled back to Gatwick International the following morning. *"'For My thoughts are not your thoughts, nor are your ways My ways,' says the Lord. 'For as the heavens are higher than the earth, so are My ways higher than your ways, and My thoughts than your thoughts'"* (Isaiah 55:8–9, NKJV).

We eventually landed back safely in Chicago and made the three-hour car journey, including stops, around the bottom of Lake Michigan to our apartment home in a small town near Grand Rapids, Michigan. God had given us the desire of our hearts to go back to Zimbabwe to see our families. *"You have given him his heart's desire, and have not withheld the request of his lips. Selah"* (Psalm 21:2, NKJV). *"Take delight in the Lord, and he will give you the desires of your heart"* (Psalm 37:4, NIV).

Year Two
Christmas Trip

Shirley, the boys and I had just returned from the 1989 Christmas and New Year's trip to close friends in Dell Rapids, South Dakota. We spent a memorable time reminiscing. Tim and Tom enjoyed sledding down a nearby snowy hill in a cardboard box with lots of thrills and spills. We soon returned refreshed for the school spring semester.

Upon my return, I was summoned to the pastor's office. The pastor's arms were folded and his face stern. The atmosphere was somber. I knew I was in trouble, but I was flummoxed. Sweat began dripping down my back.

The first semester of the second year back at the Christian school in Michigan had gone relatively well except for a run-in with two middle school girls whose influential parents were closely connected with the school board and church. I soon learned that overlapping roles could be deleterious. However, the situation ameliorated, and we moved forward.

I had struggled in my relationship with the new school board chair. I had been given full rein in the financial oversight of the school concerning the budget the previous year. The budget had balanced. However, the new chair placed a moratorium on all spending and required me to ask permission for all expenditures. Permission was difficult to obtain since we only met monthly as a school board. The micromanagement leadership style was in contrast to the delegated leadership approach of the previous board chair. I felt like I was being squeezed by a python and could hardly "breathe" as an administrator. I complied, however, albeit under duress. This reminded me of Deuteronomy 25:4: *"Do not muzzle an ox while it is treading out the grain"* (NIV).

The pastor started, "Why did you not request permission for your trip to South Dakota? It is obvious that you do not understand how we operate things here."

I explained that the contract clearly stated that I had time off over Christmas and New Year's. The pastor retorted that I was living by the "letter of the law" and not the "spirit." I was confused. I thought a contract was a contract, but now I was learning the ministry nuances and was careful not to make the same mistake in future years.

The year ground on. It became increasingly difficult to lead the school. One day, the pastor stopped me in the hallway and said, "I no longer think that you are the man for the job." This put me in conflict and sent me to my knees in prayer.

Job Search

I took the pastor at his word and dived headlong into a nationwide search for another Christian school principal position. Three schools expressed immediate interest. One was a large K-12 church school in Wisconsin, another was a midsized school in Durango, Colorado, and a third was a large Christian school in Denver, Colorado.

I was offered the position at the Wisconsin and Durango schools. I declined the position in Denver since the school was in serious debt, and I felt out of my league. Furthermore, the pastor in Durango had run off with the school's money, though the school board chairman still wanted me to come. I thought this would be going from the frying pan into the fire and declined the offer.

Despite the challenges faced at the Michigan school, I was reminded of the verse in the Bible about being a hireling. I did not want the Lord to see me as a hireling. *"But a hireling, he who is not the shepherd, one who does not own the sheep, sees the wolf coming and leaves the sheep and flees; and the wolf catches the sheep and scatters them. The hireling flees because he is a hireling and does not care about the sheep"* (John 10:12–13, NKJV).

I approached the pastor and elders with a proposition that included my staying but with the school board being changed to an advisory board. The elders said they would get back to me. They did. They unanimously approved my proposal, which included a twenty percent pay raise to match what the school in Durango had offered. The turbulent summer school search, which included hundreds of miles flying, weeks of nail-biting anticipation, and personal expense, culminated in staying at the Michigan school. We had survived two years and wondered what the third year would bring.

Year Three
Writing on the Wall
However, we went out of the frying pan and into the fire.

The pastor had a personal philosophy that any church ministry had three years to become financially self-sustaining. Since the school was a church ministry, it needed to be self-sustaining. We were now in year three of my being there. The school was sustained by school tuition and generous church support.

The support ceased abruptly after Christmas. How could we possibly be self-sustaining while struggling to pay salaries and meet basic school expenses? I immediately generated a flier for church members that invited them to sponsor a student so that we could meet expenses. I explained that we were facing a "Goliath" as we needed to meet our budget. The pastor took offense and said I was calling him "Goliath." This had not been communicated. The lack of funding was the Goliath. Still, the pastor was fuming!

Our lives went into a tailspin as we waited over the semester for the church and school board to make a final decision regarding my employment. We were in limbo.

Prophetic Marker

During this dark period, we moved from our apartment into a double-story house we hoped to purchase. It was physically moved a mile or so from its original location to a new lot—just for us. We had started the arrangements earlier with a businessman in the church, but things were not looking optimistic about the future. When my brother Liam and his wife, Penny, visited, they were appalled at the treatment we'd undergone in America in the name of Christian ministry. They thought we would be better appreciated back in Zimbabwe.

One Sunday, Dr. Mark Barclay, a visiting prophet and stranger to us, spoke at the morning service. He invited people up to the altar for prayer. Shirley went forward. God spoke to Shirley through Dr. Barclay: "Stay and don't go. Stabilize." This "word" was an answer to prayer as we seriously contemplated returning to Zimbabwe. Shirley and I understood that the Lord was saying, "Stay in America. Do not go back to Zimbabwe."

I recalled a Bible passage when I first heard God calling me to America many years before in Zimbabwe: "*But now, thus says the Lord, who created you, O Jacob, and He who formed you, O Israel: 'Fear not, for I have redeemed you; I have called you by your name; You are Mine. When you pass through the waters, I will be with you; and through the rivers, they shall not overflow you. When you walk through the fire, you shall not be burned, nor shall the flame scorch you"* (Isaiah 43:1–2, NKJV).

We now knew what to do. We had previously inquired through the Zimbabwe Embassy in Washington, D.C., about returning to Zimbabwe. However, they made it clear that one could not return to Zimbabwe after being gone for seven years. We wept. However, we saw this as further confirmation that God wanted us to stay in America.

The Bride

Shirley and I were fully immersed in the church. Shirley sang in the choir, headed up the nursery, and led a ladies' Bible study. I was a newly appointed deacon. Together we plunged into a major church play production called *The Bride*. Shirley and I each had a part and attended the frequent evening practices. Involvement in the play and encouragement from believers helped us to hold onto hope as we passed through our "black night of the soul," as St. John of the Cross had penned. A heavy oppressive cloud of uncertainty hung over us, threatening to squeeze life and joy from us. Yet the Lord kept us buoyant.

The pastor and school board finally decided to release me and look for a different principal. Ironically, I was asked to find my replacement "since you are the only one who knows what you are looking for." Incredulous.

The Lord was ever faithful and opened a door of escape to another small Christian school, this time in Lancaster, South Carolina. We connected since Roy Miles, the pastor, strongly supported Africa and missions. *"Consider it pure joy, my brothers and sisters, whenever you face trials of many kinds, because you know that the testing of your faith produces perseverance. Let perseverance finish its work so that you may be mature and complete, not lacking anything"* (1 James 1:2–4, NIV).

The Lancaster church and pastor sent a young man named Stewart Funderberg to drive our U-Haul from Michigan to Lancaster, South Carolina. We marveled at God's provision. Shirley and I and Tim and Tom followed suit. This time the Pontiac pulled a hatchback camper trailer as earlier we'd switched the utility trailer for a camper. It was another gift from God. *"Every good and perfect gift is from above..."* (James 1:17, NIV).

The prolonged icy winds and turbulence abated. God had made a way for us to *soar above the storms*. Ahead were blue skies, but on the distant horizon were telltale signs of swiftly moving sand-colored clouds....

Shirley's Reflections

I was at a prayer meeting one day when I overheard a friend saying that she was going to cut the top off her camper trailer because she did not use it anymore. She wanted a utility trailer instead. I let her know that we had a utility trailer but would like a camper trailer. We switched and charged each other one dollar for the sale.

CHAPTER 10
South Carolina
(1990-1991)

Crisis Faced: Daddy – Jesus to Me
Crisis: Health – Cancer Thief
Storm: Sandstorm – Driving Sand; Respiratory Issues

Chopper Angels

The chopper rose steadily from an open field surrounded by tall pine trees. The early morning sky was ablaze with a brilliant morning sun. The air was crisp and cool. Winds were light out of the northeast. My heart skipped a beat as the chopper suddenly tilted upward, easily clearing the pine trees. Who could believe this was a school field trip for our small Christian school in Lancaster, South Carolina? And I was the first to enjoy a 360° spin in the azure heavens above the school and surrounding pinelands—pinelands that Hurricane Hugo had ravaged several months before our arrival.

I was the principal and upper-grades teacher at the small K-5 Christian school. We were studying flight in my class. I was a proponent of making learning come alive with real experiences…and one of the parents was a local Jungle Aviation and Radio Services (JAARS) helicopter pilot, so voilà! Parents, students and even teachers were excited about the ride.

After preliminary safety tips and basic details about flying, the students and staff waited excitedly for their turn to spy the neighborhood from aloft. Thomas, our youngest, although not quite school age, was also included along with Timothy, our five-year-old son. It was a thrill, to say the least. After the final trip, we stood back from the chopper reflecting on the experience and saying goodbye to the pilot. The overhead rotor was spinning slowly with each blade easily visible. The tail rotor was still spinning at high revolutions. One could see the school grounds and building through the rotor. As the conversation with the pilot was winding down, our Tom wiggled out of my hand grip and began wandering toward the school in the direct path of the rear rotor. Thankfully, I was able to sprint toward Tom and stop him in his path. The angels were certainly working overtime that day. *"For He shall give His angels charge over you, to keep you in all your ways. In their hands they shall bear you up, lest you dash your foot against a stone"* (Psalm 91:11–12 NKJV). *Thank You, Jesus!*

Lancaster Christian School

Lancaster Christian School was a ministry of Lancaster Christian Church and picturesquely set amid woodlands surrounded by open fields and more pine woodlands on about a hundred acres. The school was a quarter of a mile down a dirt road from the country church, the personal workmanship of the pastor, a godly and quiet man with a heart for Africa and missions.

The school year progressed well. About half the school population was comprised of the nearby JAARS' and Wycliffe Bible Translators' children. The other half drew from the local population. Tim loved his teacher and excelled in kindergarten. Shirley took over as his teacher later in the year since Tim's teacher had to attend to some urgent matter.

At our graduation later that year, Timothy was draped in a white gown and cap and had both hands up praising the Lord during one of the songs. We were (and are) so proud of our son, who lives up to his name "Timothy," which means "honoring God." We're so proud of both our sons.

Our younger son, Tom, was also a delight. He would accompany Shirley to school and lightly join in class activities. His favorite part of the day was before and after school when he would explore the woods with Tim and other students. Shirley and I cautioned our sons against picking up snakes, as South Carolina was home to poisonous copperhead snakes. We explained to Tim and Tom that poisonous snakes could bite and kill you. Tom's four-year-old mind did not see the issue with this. "If I die, I'll go to heaven." We reassured Tom that this was true, but that God had plans for his life and that he should not pick up any snakes. We set clear expectations and kept an eye on the boys.

To further counter the snake issue and to convey biblical principles, I started telling the boys a made-up bedtime story. I named the protagonist Jeremiah Jeremiah and the antagonist Mrs. Copperhead. The stories continued on and off for years with events from the day woven through the story. One day Tom quipped, "Dad, that's about us." After that, the stories dwindled. *Love you, sons of the Most High God!*

Lung Cancer

Just after Christmas, I received a phone call from my brother Liam in South Africa. He had previously graduated as a medical doctor at Cape Town University and was completing a Ph.D. to boot. Our dad had flown down to Cape Town, South Africa, from his home in Zimbabwe for last-ditch medical tests. Dad had been a smoker most of his life and had lung cancer. Mom, also a smoker, accompanied him. Zimbabwe doctors feared that the cancer had metastasized throughout Dad's body. As the situation was dire, I had to arrange time off school to travel to South Africa.

Fortunately, Shirley could take over my teaching responsibilities (she had not yet replaced the kindergarten teacher). I booked a three-week ticket and flew Pan Am Airways via Charlotte and Paris to Johannesburg and Cape Town, South Africa. This was in the middle of the first Iraq War when some 1991 newspaper headlines predicted a possible third World War. Regardless, I knew this was the last opportunity I would have to see my father alive. It was still a heart-wrenching decision, and I leaned heavily on God and His Word for guidance and counsel and on Shirley's loving support.

Dad's face lit up when he saw me, and in his excitement, he scrambled to recall my name. Instead, he said, "It's the one who's come from far away!" Indeed, America was far away.

The following day Dad went with Liam for the latest test results. As he was walking in the front door, I said, "Dad, how did it go?" He replied, "It's going to rain."

I knew exactly what he meant. He knew that, medically speaking, there was no hope. A couple of days later Dad had a stroke, and his left side was mostly paralyzed. This meant he could no longer walk. I became Dad's legs and guided him from behind while he stood on my feet. Sadly, the roles had been reversed. He was no longer taking care of me as a toddler; instead, he had become the toddler, at least physically.

One morning Dad was sitting on the side of the bed with severe pain in his right side. Mom was sitting in a chair near the bed. I asked Dad if he would like prayer and asked Mom for agreement. Mom had been raised as an Irish Protestant and believed in God. However, she did not understand my "conversion" to Christ and being filled with the Spirit. She nodded sorrowfully. I placed my right hand on my dad's right side and was about to pray when my dad said, "It's hot."

I asked, "Is it hand heat?"

Dad replied, "No, it's hot. Really hot." I had not yet started praying.

"What's happening to the pain?" I inquired softly.

"The pain is leaving," Dad acknowledged.

I prayed a short but direct prayer asking God to completely remove the pain in his side and restore him to health.

For the next several days, we all enjoyed being together and making short visits to Dad's favorite places, including gazing at the Indian Ocean way below the winding Cape Town mountain roads. These were precious memories. However, soon it was time for me to escort Mom and Dad back by air to their home in the beautiful small town of Mutare, in the eastern highlands of Zimbabwe, nestled in a valley in the beautiful "Blue-Ridge" Vumba (now Bvumba) mountains about 1,500 miles north.

Dad enjoyed sitting outside in the open-back patio in a wheelchair. The chickens scratched in the dirt a short distance from the house. The house was one of the older homes in the town and was the first "school-house." It was surrounded by tall pine and oak trees and had a large mango tree at the back. Cecil John Rhodes, after whom the country of Rhodesia (now Zimbabwe) was called initially, was reported to have stopped there on one occasion.

The days were spent resting and drinking tea. Dad did not have much of an appetite for food. While sitting in his wheelchair on the outside patio, I taught him how to use his left hand to shave himself. I gently guided his hand and held a small mirror so he could see his masterpiece. We had lots of smiles and fun despite Dad's condition. The stroke had badly affected his right side, which relegated him to a wheelchair. Dad never complained. About a week later, I took the bus to Harare and flew back to Lancaster, South Carolina, and my family. My last words to my dad were, "I'll see you in June, Dad. Love you." His last words to me were, "June's not too long." Considering that it was early February 1991, there were still four and a half months before I could travel back with Shirley and the boys and visit Dad in the summer when school would be out.

While flying back to the United States on Pan Am Airways, I became aware of an incentive that the flailing airline was offering: triple bonus miles for flying and a $250 round-trip fare to England. I pondered this and wondered whether there were any restrictions. A daring plan hatched in my mind. What if… What if we—Shirley, Tim, Tom and myself—drove from our home in South Carolina to the JFK Airport in New York and flew to London, England, and back twice in one weekend? We would then have enough mileage points for "free" tickets to Kenya in Africa. One connecting flight, and we could see my dad in June in Zimbabwe as I had promised. What a thought. There must be restrictions, though.

Since arriving in the States nearly eight years prior, we'd only been able to see our families in Africa once. The prohibitive costs of air tickets meant overseas travel was infrequent, but now there was a *crazy* but possible way forward. *"Jesus looked at them and said, 'With man this is impossible, but not with God; all things are possible with God'"* (Mark 10:27, NIV).

Double Transatlantic Flights

Once home, I shared this unusual "God opportunity" with Shirley. We figured we could accrue the necessary miles to earn tickets to our destination by making the double-round trip from New York to London. Such a trip would save us thousands of dollars. We decided to take the plunge.

I called Pan Am Airways and checked. No restrictions. This was unbelievable. But it was the middle of the First Iraq War and far fewer passengers were flying for fear of being blown out of the sky by terrorists.

In my absence, Shirley taught my third- through fifth-grade class. (This was before she became Tim's kindergarten teacher a couple of months later.) She was quite adept at using the Christian Abeka curriculum and did an outstanding job during my three-week absence. She also oversaw administrative duties and wrote an excellent school newsletter. Her only complaint was that I had not left the answers to the history questions. This caused her late nights scouring the pages for answers. *Sorry, Shirley, I should have told you where the answers were.* (Perhaps this experience helped her to sail through the citizenship interview several months later.)

We made arrangements to fly two round trips to London posthaste. We planned to travel from Lancaster, South Carolina, to JFK International Airport leaving immediately after school on Friday less than one week after my return from seeing my ailing father in Zimbabwe. Our church pastor was most empathetic and supported us in our quest to earn mileage points for air tickets to Africa. He also kindly found substitutes for Monday's classes. We planned to be back teaching on Tuesday.

It was a long trip from Lancaster, South Carolina, to JFK International Airport in New York. The end of the first week in February was uncharacteristically cold, with snow and ice. This made driving somewhat treacherous, but our 1976 Pontiac Grand LeMans, which God has blessed us with, seemed to glide over ice and snow effortlessly. Fortunately, the main I-95 artery was relatively clear.

We were a couple of hours north on the I-95 interstate highway when we heard a loud "uuuaaagh" sound from the back seat. Tom was throwing up "buckets" in the back. We breathed a deep sigh. Our "cheap" tickets (which strained our small Christian school budget) were nonrefundable. I pulled off at the nearest road stop and cleaned out the back seat while Shirley comforted and cleaned Tom. What were we to do? We did not want to put Tom at risk (or others). We prayed momentarily and sensed God's peace to continue. Tom threw up a few more times before settling down. We made sure he had plenty of fluids, but he had lost his appetite somewhat.

I drove through the night, and we arrived in New York City at about 3:30 a.m. I remember driving over an almost deserted massive iron bridge with skyscrapers silhouetted against the early morning sky. I felt like I was driving on the moon, it was such an existential experience. I was in awe of how massive everything was. An hour later we arrived at JFK International Airport. A few hours later we were winging our way across the vast Atlantic Ocean.

Shirley's Uncle Bob and Auntie Betty met us at the airport late Saturday evening and brought us to their London flat not far from Heathrow International Airport where we had landed. Uncle Bob was known for playing with children and making them laugh. He picked Tim and Tom up by their ears, but I think they were too tired to find this amusing. Tom threw up on the stairs but did seem somewhat better after a while. We had a quick "cuppa" and a few light snacks before settling in for a very short night's rest. We had hardly closed our eyes when the shrill 4:00 a.m. alarm shattered our fragile sleep.

Auntie Betty fed us a light English breakfast, then Uncle Bob whisked us off to Heathrow for our early-morning departure to New York.

Jumbo Jet Baby Miracle

We were sitting in our economy class seats enjoying a hot luncheon when the captain of the jumbo 747 jet made an urgent request. Could a doctor or other medical personnel on board please come to the front of the aircraft? Shirley and I stared at each other. Both of us had some knowledge and experience in first aid. I had been a British Red Cross instructor in Zimbabwe and Shirley had completed one year of nursing school. However, our seat belts remained fastened. Someone more qualified would surely attend the emergency.

A few minutes later the captain's voice again crackled over the intercom. "Anyone having medical experience, *please* come to the front of the aircraft. There is a medical emergency on board." Shirley sprang like a leopard out of her seat without a further invitation while I remained in my seat with our two sons, wondering what the emergency might be.

During Shirley's absence from our seats, a chicken bone became lodged in my throat. Somehow the irony of this situation struck a satirical "funny bone." Shirley was up at the front of the aircraft trying to save a life, and here I was about to die from choking on a bone. How ironic. Fortunately, the bone dislodged with a cough and was propelled onto the luncheon plate.

Shirley returned from the front of the aircraft after what seemed an eternity. Her somber expression told me something was drastically wrong. "There's a little thirteen-month-old baby girl having convulsions," she gasped, her eyes moistened. "A Greek doctor is helping, but he says she won't make it. Her temperature is extremely high, and she's not breathing. They're giving her oxygen and cardiac massage. I'm helping with ice baths."

Shirley returned to the front of the aircraft. Suddenly a surge of compassion swept over me. Here we were, halfway over the Atlantic Ocean, several miles up in the atmosphere, with a dying baby on board. A strong boldness gripped me, and I stumbled to the front of the aircraft. I prayed earnestly out loud, interceding for the baby's life and speaking words of healing and faith, then slowly returned to my seat. The boys were still sleeping soundly.

Shirley remained with the baby and later told me the rest of the story. Everybody had tenaciously worked together, hanging on for the baby's life, and against hope believing for a miracle. After I had prayed fervently for the baby, Shirley prayed softly and with Holy Ghost deliberation and precision rebuked the "spirit of death" over the baby. The lifeless thirteen-month-old's body suddenly jolted as though being shocked with invisible electrical defibrillator paddles. The Greek doctor in attendance quickly removed his stethoscope and asked Shirley what she was doing.

"I'm praying," Shirley responded calmly.

"Please don't go away. We need you," the doctor pleaded.

"*The prayer of a righteous person is powerful and effective*" (James 5:16b, NIV).

Several minutes later another message from the captain informed us that the aircraft would be making an unscheduled emergency landing at a remote landing strip in Newfoundland, Canada, but that was still two hours away.

The gigantic 747 parted the ruffled clouds in preparation for landing. The leviathan-type bird touched down on the desolate snow-covered strip, its powerful jet engines in reverse thrust. The flashing lights of the ambulance met the aircraft as it taxied to a halt. It wasn't long before the jet was once again roaring toward the heavens. The intercom crackled. The relieved voice of the pilot captain announced: "The baby is out of all immediate danger." A gasp of relief escaped from the passengers.

A few hours later we arrived at New York's JFK International Airport and, because of the delay, had to run to our connecting flight for our second round trip over the Atlantic to London and back. The same passport attendant surprisedly said, "Didn't I see you yesterday?" We quickly explained what we were doing and were ushered through without fanfare. Both boys were doing well. Tom was doing much better health-wise by now. Lots of prayers. Lots of liquids. No more throwing up. *Thank You, Jesus!* "*They will take up serpents; and if they drink anything deadly, it will by no means hurt them; they will lay hands on the sick, and they will recover*" (Mark 16:18, NKJV).

The second Atlantic round trip from New York to London and back was uneventful. We had a relatively short turnaround in London and about twenty hours later returned to JFK International Airport in New York. Now we had the drive to our friends Neil and Noline's home for an overnight stop. They had relocated to Shippensburg, Pennsylvania, and were involved with Marriage Ministries International. They were expecting us for a late dinner.

I was exhausted from almost four days without meaningful sleep, but we eventually made it to Neil and Noline's at 2:00 a.m. *Thank You, Jesus.* "*Cast all your anxiety on him because he cares for you*" (1 Peter 5:7, NIV). "*Truly my soul finds rest in God; my salvation comes from him*" (Psalm 62:1, NIV).

The overnight and morning stop with our friends was restorative. After a hearty breakfast and some "ol' time" reminiscing and fellowship with our former pastor and his wife, now our good friends, it was time to hit the road back to Lancaster, South Carolina.

The drive back was uneventful. Mission accomplished. We had flown twice over the Atlantic Ocean in one weekend and racked up triple mileage points. These could be used however we chose, but the purpose was to go and see my dad in Zimbabwe in June 1991. It was now the middle of February. Time was of the essence, as doctors had given up hope since the cancer had metastasized throughout his body.

Tulips in Heaven

Two weeks after our transatlantic crossings and three weeks after my return from Africa, my youngest brother, Liam, a medical doctor, called me. It was early in the morning, and we were just setting off to school. I knew intuitively what the call was about. God had graciously prepared my heart in a dream the evening before. I saw my father alive and well, a gardener in the most beautiful garden filled with red and yellow tulips. He was divinely content in his new heavenly home. Dad loved gardening.

The shrill ring of the house phone arrested my attention. "Martin, Dad passed away this morning at 8:15 a.m. He died peacefully in his sleep." My inner world became very quiet. The shock of Dad's passing seeped into my brain. I sat, momentarily numbed, but not caught unawares. We had tried so hard to be able to make it back to Africa in June, but this was February 25, 1991. June was still a while off. Alas.

Liam went on to recount Dad's last conversation with Mom as told by our sister, Mary. Mom and Dad were sitting on the side of the bed the evening before when Dad became quiet before imploring Mom to let him go. Mom had previously confided that she could not let Dad go for fear of being alone. She hated being alone. Dad persisted. Mom and Dad then sang a hymn, "Abide with Me," and Mom said, "I commit you into the hands of Jesus." Dad soon fell asleep and never awoke. He died peacefully. "*Yea, though I walk through the valley of the shadow of death, I will fear no evil: for thou art with me; thy rod and thy staff they comfort me*" (Psalm 23:4, KJV). *Thank You, Jesus, for my daddy*. He was like Jesus to me in his humility and servanthood. He was not perfect, but he was a good man. Not rich. A family man. An amazing father. A hard worker. Impeccably dressed for work—but not in the garden. A gentle individual. Kind. A great storyteller. So good with little children—and chickens. Athletic. He loved my mother. He loved God and was faithful at church. A slow driver. A good listener. Understanding. What a heritage.

Bootie

I went to school as usual that day, taught my students and did my principal duties. It was a tough day, but God's grace brought me through it. Upon my arrival home, we sent the boys outside to play with Bootie, our dog. The boys loved playing with Bootie.

A neighboring farmer gave us Bootie a few months back. The farmer was well in his eighties, grew all his own vegetables, and plowed with two mules. He offered us "maayders," which we soon discovered were delicious red tomatoes about the size of a baseball.

Bootie had a habit of visiting his former owner. This meant crossing the narrow country road where cars were prone to speeding.

Shortly after my arrival home, we were alerted by a car's screeching tires and screams from outside. Tim came dashing inside and said, "He's been hit! He's been hit!" We thought that *Tom* had been hit by a car. We dashed outside. To our extreme relief, our sons were fine. They knew not to play near the road.

They quickly recounted how Bootie had been run over by a car. Bootie had run across the road directly in front of a lady driving by. It was an accident. Somehow, he clawed his way up the embankment to our home and onto the front porch. It was very evident that the force of the vehicle had crushed Bootie's skull. Crimson blood streamed from his ears and eyes. We were devastated.

A local veterinarian took Bootie's pain away...permanently. The driver who had hit Bootie graciously paid for the procedure. We buried Bootie in the backyard and held a brief "doggie" service.

I felt the strangest peace. Somehow, being forced to deal with Bootie's traumatic injury and subsequent death helped me to accept and cope with having lost my father earlier that day. It was as though God had wrapped His arms around me. I was abiding in His peace. "*Abide in Me, and I in you. As the branch cannot bear fruit of itself, unless it abides in the vine, neither can you, unless you abide in Me*" (John 15:4, NKJV). "*He who dwells in the secret place of the Most High shall abide under the shadow of the Almighty. I will say of the Lord, 'He is my refuge and my fortress; my God, in Him I will trust'*" (Psalm 91:1–2, NIV).

Moving Again

The ensuing days turned into weeks and months. Soon it was graduation time. We held the graduation in the campus church building with parents in full attendance. Kindergarteners were graduating to first grade and fifth graders to sixth grade and middle school. Timothy stood tall and proud. During the praise and worship part of the ceremony, he raised both arms to God and praised Him unashamedly. Oh, the innocence of a child. How tender. We could see God's hand on Tim's life and rejoiced over God's goodness shining through our son as he honored God. *"For this reason I have sent to you Timothy, my son whom I love, who is faithful in the Lord"* (1 Corinthians 4:17a, NIV).

About half the school population was comprised of JAARS and Wycliffe students. The Jungle Aviation and Relay Services started in 1948. Wycliffe Bible Translators, which was founded in 1942, was named after John Wycliffe, the English scholar and theologian. Their goal is to translate the Bible into every known tongue. Conversations with these parents were always invigorating and humbling. They had given up everything for the cause of Christ and were following Him by faith. Toward the end of the school year, we became aware that several parents were being deployed overseas. This meant their children would be going with them, which in turn meant our small school population would be cut in half. The school could no longer afford a principal. I was offered a teacher's job and a small salary that did not meet our needs. We would have to move after only one year in Lancaster, South Carolina.

Job Search…Again

I had attended a Christian School Administrators' conference in Columbia, South Carolina, and met a fellow Christian school principal named Robert. His experiences mirrored my own in so many respects, yet he stayed true to God's calling on his life. I was encouraged.

Through a God-ordained series of events, Shirley and the boys and I "hitched up our chariot" (our small camper trailer) and traveled from South Carolina, through the Bronx, to upstate New York, then back through Shippensburg, Pennsylvania, and to Lancaster, South Carolina, again. It was an all-out effort to secure a better position that would meet our needs. The trip was an adventure. We were confident that God would guide our footsteps. *"Trust in the Lord with all your heart, and lean not on your own understanding; in all your ways acknowledge Him, and He shall direct your paths"* (Proverbs 3:5–6, NKJV).

School administrator/principal job offers had quickly poured in from Columbia, South Carolina, the Bronx and upstate New York. Our lifelong friend and pastor also had connected us with a church ministry in Shippensburg that had a crisis pregnancy center. I interviewed with them.

I had never thought of being a director of a crisis pregnancy center. This was completely out of my comfort zone. So was the coffee we were offered as we waited in a small waiting area neatly adorned with potted plants. I "watered" a nearby plant with the strong black brew, as I did not want to appear ungrateful for the coffee. I was offered the position here, too. The expectation was that Shirley would volunteer in the adjoining Christian bookstore, which was supposed to funnel funds to the crisis pregnancy center. Other funds came from fundraising and support from area churches.

We made our way back to South Carolina with much to talk, think and pray about. Which of the four job offers did the Lord want us to accept? Where would the best fit be? Where could our children flourish? No sooner were we back home in South Carolina when the pastor of the church school in Columbia, South Carolina, encouraged me to come down for a week and see for myself what the school was like. I agreed.

Simple Faith, Profound Consequences

I fell in love with the school. I could see myself fitting in. I was in my element. The pastor and school staff were wonderful. The church was a good fit, as the pastor preached the Word of God. By this time Shirley and I had agreed that the offers could be whittled to two options: the crisis pregnancy center in Pennsylvania, where our former pastor and friend resided, or the Christian school in Columbia, South Carolina. We were both leaning strongly toward the Columbia, South Carolina, offer. However, midweek during my absence from Shirley and while I was undergoing a trial week at the school in Columbia, we both decided to inquire of the Lord for *His* confirmation. We asked the Lord for a confirming scripture verse.

The Holy Spirit honored our request. We each received a confirming "word" from the Lord midweek: Pennsylvania. Wow! My experience with Christian schools to date had been turbulent, and I was somewhat leery of Christian schools and ministry in general. Still, we both wanted to accept the Christian school in our heads, but our spirits said otherwise. "'*For I know the plans I have for you,*' declares the Lord, '*plans to prosper you and not to harm you, plans to give you hope and a future'"* (Jeremiah 29:11, NIV).

We started packing and prepared to go to Pennsylvania. A semi-truck driver in our Lancaster church had an empty truck going to Pennsylvania. He offered to transport our belongings free of charge. He left the semitruck at our home so we could pack at our leisure. The day before we were to leave for Pennsylvania, the Columbia, South Carolina, pastor called and implored us to "turn the semi around; there's still time." He believed I was the person to head the school and liked Shirley and me. We were torn. We desperately wanted to turn the van around and follow our heads and hearts, but we had prayed and received a "word" from the Lord for Pennsylvania. It seemed to us that the Lord was leading us to Pennsylvania. We made the agonizing decision to stay on course for the unfamiliar crisis pregnancy center position in Pennsylvania. *"Teach me to do Your will, for You are my God; let Your good Spirit lead me on level ground"* (Psalm 143:10, NASB). *"And he said, Abba, Father, all things are possible unto thee; take away this cup from me: nevertheless not what I will, but what thou wilt"* (Mark 14:36, KJV).

Crisis center, here we come. We were taking God at His Word and rising *above the storms* of life's direction. Yet there were hints of a low-pressure system and cold Atlantic air colliding with interior air along the east coast....

Shirley's Reflections

Our year in South Carolina was most enjoyable. Of all the states we had lived in, this was the most beautiful climate. We lived two hours from the ocean and two hours from the mountains. Beautiful relationships were formed. It was a healing balm to be out from under the difficulties we had endured for three years in Michigan. It was a time of healing.

CHAPTER 11

Pennsylvania Early Days

(1991-1995)

Crisis Faced: Career Change – Ministering to Those in Crisis
Crisis: Legal Crisis – Defending the Unborn
Storm: Nor'easter – Strong Winds, Heavy Precipitation

Arrival

Everything changed in Shippensburg, Pennsylvania: new job, new boss, new church, new friends, new school for Tim and Tom. However, it was reassuring to reconnect with our former pastor Neil and his wife, Noline, our forever friends, from Zimbabwe. *So proud of you, Neil and Noline. Shirley and I are so honored to still be counted as your friends.*

Up until our move to Pennsylvania in America, I had been involved in Christian school ministry, first as an elementary teacher in Sioux Falls, South Dakota, then as the principal and a teacher near Grand Rapids, Michigan, and Lancaster, South Carolina. Now it was different. The boys boarded a bus for a forty-minute commute to a large Christian school in nearby Chambersburg, Pennsylvania.

It was hard to let go of my former direct influence on the boys' education. I was (and still am) a passionate proponent of Christian school education and excellence. I understood from the Scriptures that parents are directly responsible for their children's education, especially their spiritual education, and that they were to "...*bring them up in the training and admonition of the Lord*" (Ephesians 6:4, NKJV). Other Scriptures also reinforced this mindset: "*Train up a child in the way he should go, and when he is old he will not depart from it*" (Proverbs 22:6, NKJV); "*Sanctify them by Your truth. Your word is truth*" (John 17:17, NKJV); "*In whom are hidden all the treasures of wisdom and knowledge*" (Colossians 2:3, MEV); "*Beware lest anyone captivate you through philosophy and vain deceit, in the tradition of men and the elementary principles of the world, and not after Christ*" (Colossians 2:8, MEV).

Shirley and I continued to closely monitor our sons' academic progress and to work with them on their homework. Still, our lives had changed. My "school" was the community and beyond, helping my audience to understand the devastating consequences of terminating life within the womb and the hope and practical help that were available to those affected by unplanned pregnancies. It also involved direct counseling and oversight of seventy-plus volunteers.

My first few days on the job involved "volunteer" training to help me understand the scope and intent of the ministry. I was completely unfamiliar with crisis pregnancy centers or even abortion. These terms soon became very familiar to me. Furthermore, I blushed when talking about such terms as *pregnancy* and related words. However, I soon embraced the vision of helping those in crisis pregnancy and standing for the unborn child.

Pan Am

A couple of weeks after our arrival in Shippensburg, I had a gnawing feeling in my gut. "*Call Pan Am.*" I wanted to dismiss the feeling, but I sensed the Lord may be trying to tell me something. The feeling persisted. In the natural, there was no need to call the airline. The mileage points we had earned flying over the Atlantic Ocean twice in one weekend several months earlier were good for a few years. The pressing need to use the points to fly back to Zimbabwe to visit my ailing father had evaporated since my father had graduated to glory. So, why call?

I called. The Pan Am representative quickly confirmed the accuracy of the Lord's prompting.

"You have two weeks to use your mileage points. Use them or lose them. Pan Am will no longer be operating." Wow. What a shock. *Thank You, Jesus, for the heads-up.* "*For as many as are led by the Spirit of God, these are sons of God*" (Romans 8:14, NKJV).

Shirley and I faced the reality of the mileage points expiring. This was out of our control. I had just started a new job and could not afford to take time off work. The boys had just started a new school. Shirley had begun "volunteering" at the bookstore, a fundraising ministry for the crisis pregnancy center. Despite the harsh realities, we decided that Shirley and the boys should make a ten-day trip to Zimbabwe to visit her parents and made last-minute arrangements.

This was a whirlwind trip for Shirley and the boys with some scary moments without Dad. However, they finally arrived at Shirley's hometown of Bulawayo.

The next several days were a blur for them but were a wonderful opportunity for Shirley to reconnect with her parents and the boys to get to know their grandparents a little. The boys were still young enough to ride on their grandpa's back while he crawled across the carpet in the living room. However, he had raised girls, not full-blooded all-American energetic boys. He was soon exhausted. Poor grandpa. One cultural misunderstanding remains etched in the boys' and Shirley's minds. Grandpa told them not to pick any "pawpaws." This was the British-African name for fruit like papayas. There were several tall "pawpaw" trees near the outside "kia," a small apartment for live-in servants. The boys found a yellow pawpaw on the ground, and Tim picked it up to show Shirley. Grandpa thought they were disobedient, but they were merely inquisitive five- and six-almost-seven-year-olds who did not understand the African terms "pawpaw" and "kia."

Things soon settled down. It was a learning process for everyone. *Grandpa, we love you. We know this was a big adjustment for you, too. Thank you for the fun times you and Shirley and the boys had together. Sorry about the "paw paws."*

Before long, Shirley and the boys were back in Shippensburg, Pennsylvania, and life resumed its "new normal" routine. Shirley worked in the bookstore, the boys were bused to and from school, and I headed up the crisis pregnancy center. We all went to church on Sunday mornings.

Crisis Pregnancy Center Stories
No Junk

I worked as the director of the crisis pregnancy center for four years. The center dealt with every conceivable crisis, not just crisis pregnancies. Several crisis events come to mind.

The outgoing director and founder of the crisis pregnancy center, plus Shirley and I, traveled to a client's home in the remote Appalachian hills. Jen (not her real name) was a rotund and effervescent lady surrounded by active children who clamored for her attention like busy bees. She was patient and welcoming. Upon our arrival at her tiny home tucked into the side of a mountain, I noticed a piece of paper stuck on the living room wall with the words, "I must be somebody 'cause God don't make no junk." I marveled at the truth in these words and how they mirrored Psalm 139:13–14: "*For you created my inmost being; you knit me together in my mother's womb. I praise you because I am fearfully and wonderfully made; your works are wonderful, I know that full well*" (NIV).

Jen offered us tea and cookies. The cookies tasted delicious, but we had to overlook the scurrying cockroaches and broken-down couch and chairs. Later we helped Jen move to a nice apartment in town. She continued to "make babies" as a single mother despite counsel to the contrary. It seemed that state funding had its appeal, and she knew how to manage the system. Still, she was a delightful soul and often reached out to us for help.

Snakes and Rats

Another early experience included rescuing a lady and her several children from an abusive situation. The lady had called our hotline for help, and we responded. The former director still had an active presence in the ministry and accompanied some volunteers, Shirley, and me to the mother in distress. We drove into the picturesque fall colors of the countryside with hills in the background. As we rounded one corner, a large white house graced the landscape at the bottom of a hill. However, looks can be deceiving, as we would soon discover.

We entered the home through the front door. The rooms were dark and damp. The kitchen ceiling tiles bulged with water from recent rains and were blackened underneath with mold. Once our eyes became accustomed to the dim light, it seemed that the walls were moving with critters. Snakes and rats infested the walls. Several smaller children appeared, some in soggy diapers, and all with green extraneous matter dripping from their noses. What a pitiful sight and existence. The stench of humanity and filth was overpowering, causing some to retch. Despite her circumstances, the lady kindly offered us tea, which we politely refused. She also made oatmeal for the kids for breakfast, which was crawling with weevils. We extracted the lady and her children and took them to a safe place.

The next day, I had an unplanned meeting. A tall, brutish-looking, strong man pounded angrily on the only door to my tiny office. He loudly asked if I was the director and demanded to know where his family was. He then looked out the window at my parked 1976 Grand LeMans Pontiac.

"Is that yours?" he demanded gruffly.

"Yes," I responded calmly. "That is my vehicle."

"How would you feel if I smashed the windshield with a baseball bat?"

By this time, Shirley had become aware of the scene and alerted the fire station next door—just in case.

The Holy Spirit helped me to respond in a calm manner to this dangerously angry man. "Where are you hurting, sir?" The words just flowed. The man collapsed in tears and bawled like a baby. "*A gentle answer turns away wrath, but a harsh word stirs up anger*" (Proverbs 15:1, NIV). "*If the anger of the ruler rises against you, do not leave your place, for calmness will lay great offenses to rest*" (Ecclesiastes 10:4, ESV, emphasis added).

Sherry Lee (Not Her Real Name)

There were many other stories like the pregnant teenager who saw our materials at her school and decided not to abort her baby. However, the last impressionable client crisis came in the form of a lady in her mid-thirties. We will call her Sherry Lee. Sherry Lee was beautiful on the outside but shattered on the inside. She had been a believer in her youth but married into verbal and physical abuse. She had reached rock bottom and came to us for counsel. Sherry Lee was faithful in keeping

131

her appointments and evidence of her healing displayed itself as she blossomed like a fresh rose filled with vitality. She rededicated her life to Christ and continued to grow in His Word.

On Easter Saturday, 1995, I was attending a Dick Mills breakfast with Neil (my pastor friend) in nearby Harrisburg, Pennsylvania. Dick was acclaimed worldwide for his accuracy in dispensing words of knowledge with accompanying Scriptures. He pointed to Neil and spoke about God moving him in ministry. To me, he spoke about God's ability in me for writing. A few months later, Neil moved to Colorado (a ministry promotion). Several years later I began my doctoral work and then completed a book based on my work—a period of about ten years' worth of writing. I marvel at the power of God's Word spoken with humility and power. *Thank you for your obedience, Dick Mills. I am still writing.*

I received a phone call during this breakfast meeting from Sherry Lee's in-laws. Sherry Lee had driven into the back of a semitruck and was in a coma in the hospital. Her brain had become detached from its stem. She was not expected to make it through the night. I prayed. She had come such a long way. Sherry Lee entered heaven's gates the following day, Easter Sunday. I wept. "*And He said, 'Where have you laid him?' They said to Him, 'Lord, come and see.' Jesus wept. Then the Jews said, 'See how He loved him!'*" (John 11:34–36, NKJV).

Hold-up

One day I received a call from my boss. "Martin, a gunman is holding up Kmart. I think you should get down there to offer counseling to any hostages who are released."

I flew to my vehicle but not before calling Shirley to tell her where I was going. Shirley was naturally alarmed and promised to pray.

I pulled into the parking lot of a building directly across the road from Kmart where local emergency crews were beginning to assemble. I was quickly assimilated into the crisis management team. Hopefully there would be no shooting, since we could be in the line of fire from the gunman.

We understood from initial reports that a man armed with a shotgun was holding hostages. Later we learned that the man's wife had walked out on him that morning. It was obvious that the man was hurting deeply. My heart was to go and talk to him and share Jesus' compassion, but the police had cordoned off the area.

Those who had managed to escape the store were directed to the makeshift emergency center. I was able to greet and comfort both men and women and offer prayer. Tears flowed from many. This was an enormous shock to the system. Who would have thought that such a thing could happen in small-town Pennsylvania? Slowly hostages were released one by one and directed to the makeshift crisis center. Many welcomed the counseling and prayer.

The impasse continued for about five hours. Eventually the gunman gave himself up and was quickly descended upon by droves of armed SWAT team responders. This was a day marked in infamy and deep inner pain. Fortunately, no one had been hurt physically. Sadly, the emotional wounds may still linger to this day. *"He heals the brokenhearted and binds up their wounds"* (Psalm 147:3, NIV). *"The Spirit of the Lord is upon me, because he hath anointed me to preach the gospel to the poor; he hath sent me to heal the brokenhearted, to preach deliverance to the captives, and recovering of sight to the blind, to set at liberty them that are bruised, to preach the acceptable year of the Lord"* (Luke 4:18–19, KJV).

Perspective Articles and Community Outreach

Working for the crisis pregnancy center afforded me opportunities to meet interesting people. My boss introduced me to Jim, the local newspaper editor, and arranged with him for me to write a weekly newspaper column to promote the crisis pregnancy center.

I wrote the weekly newspaper column for almost four years. The columns covered topics ranging from abortion to various crises and how to overcome them with faith in Christ.

Jim and I became friends. We often played tennis at the local university tennis courts. I also played racquetball there. Later Jim and his wife became close family friends. Jim was unashamed of his faith in Christ and would evidence this in the editorial part of the weekly newspaper. His famous "one-liner" was "never let the facts stand in the way of a good story." He was joking, of course, and held to the highest integrity and accuracy in the newspaper world.

Community Outreach and Backlash

A local community pastor sympathetic to the plight of the unborn offered his youth group to distribute pro-life literature at the local middle and high schools. The day was set with the youth group. Some were middle schoolers and others high schoolers—a perfect balance. I made research-based "educational" materials available to students who distributed these to their peers. Reports were immediate and impacting. High school students were apparently crying after seeing the materials. One student showed the papers to her science teacher and demanded to know if it was true. Was abortion murder? The science teacher reportedly tossed the papers in the garbage and said, "You cannot trust everything you read."

I returned home to a "boatload" of landline messages on our answering machine. One message was from an individual who promised to sue me. I could tell from the tone and intensity of the message that he was not joking. It felt like I had been sucker punched in the abdomen. As an educator who was now passionate about the lives of the unborn and their parents, I was trying to "educate" the public so they could make an informed decision on abortion. I started to realize that this was a volatile topic and that most people had their minds made up and shut like a bank vault.

I expected Shirley to empathize with my "poor me" plight. Instead, she told me to "toughen up" and fight for the unborn. They were worth it. The unexpected firm "kick in the pants" jolted me to the present reality and the need to persevere and weather the storm for the sake of the unborn and the gospel. My resolve to share the love of Jesus and the truth about abortion deepened.

Jim, my editor friend, was elated. His newspaper and newspapers in neighboring counties and beyond were carrying the news of a crisis pregnancy center director who "knew exactly what he was doing" by having youth distribute materials in the local schools. This incident sparked much regional newspaper coverage and controversy over the next several weeks.

Television Debate

During this time, and as a direct result of the youth blitz, I received an invitation from the local university, Shippensburg University, to debate the president of a local chapter of Planned Parenthood, a national pro-abortion agency.

My pastor told me, "It's not enough to know there is a devil. You need to know who it is." The "enemy" soon surfaced in the form of the senior clergyman of a local denominational church. How could a person of the cloth support the killing of selfless and totally harmless unborn children? "*The god of this age has blinded the minds of unbelievers, so that they cannot see the light of the gospel that displays the glory of Christ, who is the image of God*" (2 Corinthians 4:4, NIV).

The debate was televised live on campus. The moderator asked us to state our positions. I was directed to go first.

"I am pro-choice," I began. "My choice is life." I continued, "I believe life begins at conception. The baby's brain waves can be detected after three weeks and its heartbeat after six weeks."

I then showed the moderator and TV audience a life-size model of a nine- to ten-week-old unborn baby, about the size of my pinkie finger. "An unborn baby at just two and a half months of age has everything it needs for life. It just needs a safe place to grow until it is time to be born. Sadly, the most unsafe place for an unborn baby is in its mother's womb with abortion killing one in three unborn children. The unborn baby is not given any anesthetic even though it's proven that babies in the womb feel pain. They are ripped apart and suctioned from their mother's womb." I paused and the moderator responded by directing his comments to the president of Planned Parenthood.

"Is that true, Reverend? Does life begin at conception?"

"Yes, life begins at conception," the reverend responded.

"So, you agree with Mr. Ratcliffe's position? Doesn't that mean that children are being murdered?"

I was shocked. I was on a secular university campus with the moderator taking my side. It seemed that he was in disbelief.

The Planned Parenthood reverend clarified. "I agree that life begins at conception. The question is, what kind of life is it?"

It is hard to imagine how highly intelligent human beings can be so ignorant. Really?

"Hens lay eggs and chicks are hatched. When you sow carrot seeds, you get carrots. The human embryo produces a human, not a cat or a fish or a mouse," I responded articulately and respectfully but with a measure of incredulity.

The debate ended soon enough. I felt the Holy Spirit had enabled me to be His ambassador for the unborn child and his or her mother (and father). I felt as though I was fighting for my life and the lives of countless potential abortion victims.

My Conception

I reflected on my own beginning. I was conceived and born out of wedlock. My mother yielded me to a foster family while she spent a year in the hospital recovering from tuberculosis. I'm not sure where my father was during my first eighteen months, but my earliest pictures show me in the loving arms of my mother and father. I thank my mother for not aborting me. She went through the pain and embarrassment of carrying me for nine months in an era when pregnant unwed mothers were shunned by society. It would have been easier to have eliminated the "problem."

Thank you, Mom, for your courage in giving birth to Martin James Alexander Ratcliffe. Your decision to carry me to term and not abort me has resulted in my marriage to Shirley, our two amazing sons and their wonderful wives and five incredible grandchildren, all full of life and all living for God. As a result of saving my life, many lives have literally been saved from physical, emotional and spiritual death. Your one decision to let me live has given the gift of life to others. I am eternally grateful for your very courageous life-giving decision. So proud of you. Thank you, Mom. Love you.

"*Before I formed you in the womb I knew you, before you were born I set you apart; I appointed you as a prophet to the nations*" (Jeremiah 1:5, NIV).

First Owned Home

Shirley and I were elated when we "qualified" for a low-income housing loan. My take-home pay from the crisis center was about half a teacher's income, and Shirley was not paid for "volunteering" in the crisis center's bookstore. It seemed unlikely that we would ever own our own home, but we believed (and still believe) in the God of miracles.

We had put an offer on an acre lot in farmland country a couple of miles outside of Shippensburg. The immediate neighbors were nice enough and the nearby Mennonite farmers were welcoming. Despite some neighborly opposition to the "small" size of our home (under 1,100 square feet, but with an unfinished basement), we were eventually approved for the home loan.

Shirley and I flew to England for a week to use my Pan Am mileage points during the building phase of the home. "Uncle Neil" and "Auntie Noline" looked after the boys. We visited longtime friends Tony and Nancy in England, plus Shirley's Auntie Betty and Uncle Bob in London. Soon after our arrival back in Pennsylvania, we moved into our modest home, complete with a white picket fence.

How wonderful to own our own little home at last. We were flying *above the storms*. We thought peaceful days and *warmer* temperatures were on the way. Alas, a large region of cold rotating air was strengthening....

Shirley's Reflections

I think that of all the jobs I have ever held, managing the Christian bookstore has been the most rewarding. The majority of my clientele were Amish or Mennonite. I have always had a love for reading and usually read one book a week. I met many genuine, godly people and was able to pray for them when they had needs.

When I first started working in the bookstore, I found out that it was deep in debt. I worked hard to pay off the debt and did so in just ten months. I had been told that when it was debt-free, I would be salaried. I worked for four years without remuneration before I eventually became the owner. I then participated in student textbook buybacks, which really helped with income.

CHAPTER 12

Pennsylvania Later Days

(1993-1997)

Crisis Faced: Unmet Expectations
Crisis: Relationship – Severed Bond
Storm: Polar Vortex – Frigid Temperatures

Tim and Tom

Tim and Tom loved the outdoors. A 120-foot by 30-foot wide ridge of trees separated our back boundary line from a neighboring farmer's plowed field. The tree ridge was filled with red and black raspberry bushes and was an exciting place to explore. The boys and I built a tree house in the middle of the tree ridge. The base of the floor was ten feet off the ground and the slanted roof was seventeen feet at its highest point. We included a trapdoor and a rope for easy "escape," plus horizontal wooden reinforcement slats that doubled as a step ladder. Bill, a handyman missionary friend, kindly made finishing adjustments to the imposing structure. The boys and I then painted the tree house.

Shirley climbed the "steps" up the tree house to hang pictures for the boys. However, once inside, she was overcome with paint fumes and could hardly breathe. I quickly helped Shirley to *terra firma*. She felt like she was choking on air and "collapsed" at the nearby picnic table. It took half an hour or so for her to regain her normal breathing rhythm.

Tim and Tom begged us to spend the night in the tree house. So, a couple of nights later (once the paint fumes had subsided), they clambered up the tree house steps with all their "camping" gear. Fortunately, it was still summer, so the evenings were warm. However, summer was also the rainy season. At about 11:00 p.m. we heard thunder rumbling and then shrill shrieks pierced the darkness as two sets of feet scampered down the tree house steps and came running across the back lawn to the back door. "Thunder, thunder," they yelled. At just five and seven years of age, Tom and Tim had not been exposed to the "raw" elements by themselves. They soon settled into their own beds and never ventured to spend another night in the tree house again.

Tim and Tom caught the school bus to a Christian school in Chambersburg, about a forty-minute ride away. They seemed to be so young riding the bus such a distance. Sometimes we would pick Tom up from the bus while he slept. Once when Tom became bored, he started chewing on the back of the bus seat. When the principal asked why he had torn the seat, he responded that he was hungry. Regardless, he had to pay for the "food." We insisted that he pay his debt in one-dollar bills so he could grasp the import of his actions.

Overall, our boys did well academically at school and won first-place prizes at the annual Association of Christian Schools International (ACSI) speaking contests. *Well done, sons! Your mom and I are so proud of you.*

Once school was out for the day and homework was finished, Tim and Tom would shoot arrows with their newly acquired bows. They also enjoyed playing with the neighbors. One adjacent neighbor, "Miss Diane," was a middle-aged woman who truly loved Tim and Tom. The boys often ventured to her home and were fed ice cream and other treats. Miss Diane's husband introduced the boys to Western movies. Once Miss Diane gave Tim a "birthday box" gift. The larger outer box contained several successively smaller boxes all gift-wrapped. Tim eagerly opened each box, but to his dismay did not find a gift. However, with a little encouragement to "reexamine" each gift, he found several dollar bills hidden in the wrapping. He was elated.

On snowy days, the boys and I sledded down "Karper's Hill." Mr. Karper was a neighbor on a hill with a dirt road running down to the main blacktop country road. When the snow was compact and icy, it was slick and ideal for the quarter-mile rush to the main road. Careful last-minute steering averted any collisions with cars on the main road.

On other days, the boys and I would go cross-country skiing. Sometimes the snow was packed two feet or more above the asphalt. A kind Mennonite farmer would use his tireless tractor-plow and clear the roads. The only problem was that the snow piled up several feet at the end of our driveway. A few hours of early morning snow shoveling did the trick and cleared a path from our house to the road. It was exhausting.

Tim and Tom loved the Mennonite farmer and his family. The farmer treated them much like his own children and gave them rides on the huge Clydesdale farm horse plus rides on his cows. Shirley passed on the boys' plain-colored pants or shirts that might be compatible with Mennonite attire. We often purchased their mouth-watering home-baked goodies and fruit from their trees.

I volunteered as the soccer coach for the boys' local community soccer team. Tim and Tom became quite skilled and played for their high school varsity teams in later years. Tim was even the soccer team captain. They both became accomplished soccer players.

Bookstore

Shirley transitioned from bookstore manager to owner after a deal was agreed upon with the seller. We borrowed the loan amount from a kind businessman we had met while singing at an area Full Gospel Businessmen's meeting. After we made a good-faith effort and had paid back a portion, he graciously canceled our remaining debt. We were elated and humbled by this very kind gesture. *"A generous person will prosper; whoever refreshes others will be refreshed"* (Proverbs 11:25, NIV). *Thank You, Jesus!*

Shirley worked tirelessly over the next fifteen months and the bookstore grew slowly. However, there were many challenges. Churches would bypass the local Christian bookstore in favor of reduced prices with chain bookstores and Christian book distributors. The bitter winter of 1994-1995 did not help as sidewalks had to be de-iced and cleared. Hotel construction in our block was also underway. There were now fewer patrons. It was also challenging for the boys to be dropped off at Shirley's Christian bookstore instead of at home. We finally decided to "sell" the bookstore.

A church in nearby Chambersburg was interested in the store. We agreed on a ninety-day "trial" period. On day eighty-nine, I drove to the church to conclude business on behalf of Shirley and met with the prospective new bookstore owners.

We had so many hopes and dreams tied up in the bookstore. We hoped God could prosper us through this business and now in an all-but-final sale. We had taken the risk and had acquired thousands of dollars' worth of merchandise before deciding to sell. We were hoping to recoup costs and reinvest profits into the student book buyback portion of the store, which we had retained separately. We were grateful for our small crisis pregnancy income but recognized that with growing sons were growing family needs. We were hoping to supplement our income.

"We've decided to not go through with the bookstore deal. Some members don't like that the bookstore is open on Sundays."

These were not the words I was expecting. This was day eighty-nine, just hours away from day ninety. My world shattered. And later Shirley's world shattered, too. The time lapse would not allow us to sell the aging merchandise at a profit (if we could find a buyer). That day I realized that day eighty-nine is not day ninety. A deal is not a deal until it's a deal! Valuable life lesson! Painful. So painful!

I drove home sedately, my mind and emotions whirring. My heart was heavy with grief. I pulled off the side of the road and grabbed a pen and paper. I scribbled down a song and later put a melody to it. The song was titled, "You Can't Take It With You." The song told the story of what had happened but through the lens of learning and God's amazing love. One chorus line went, "You can't take it with you, you've got to let it go." One verse had these lyrics:

Now letting go's not easy, it can really hurt
To see your prized possessions crumbling in the dirt
But if you'll look toward heaven, Jesus you will see
He'll give you strength and victory

I knew we had to "carry on." Somehow God would make a way for us where there seemed to be no way. After all, He was and is the Way Maker.

We ended up vastly reducing everything and selling the bookstore content to the owner of another small Christian bookstore. We had her sign a contract that we would be paid if ever she went bankrupt. We only asked for a percentage of what she made each month until we had been paid in full. Unfortunately, she had not told us that her bookstore was struggling financially, and she eventually claimed bankruptcy. However, it was a no-assets bankruptcy, and we lost everything. Whatever assets there were had to go to lawyer fees.

We retained the college textbook buyback portion of the bookstore and relocated to a small, rented place closer to the local university. Students from the university sold their used textbooks to us, and we returned them to the appropriate company for a fair profit. Income from this part of the business kept us buoyant over the next few months. *Thank You, Jesus!*

Church and Ministry

I was intimately involved with our church, the crisis center and later the Christian publishing company that my pastor and boss also owned and ran. He invited me to pioneer workbooks for authors he serviced. I wrote several workbooks for three well-known Christian teachers and preachers of the time.

Shirley and I became friends with Larry and Juliana Walker shortly after they arrived in Shippensburg. Larry worked as a ghostwriter for the publishing business. He was a top-notch writer who transformed audio or written verbiage into masterpiece books. We experienced life together. *Larry and Juliana, you were and are a blessing to Shirley and me. You live Jesus.*

Crisis End

The crisis center struggled to support itself and was unexpectedly closed. I felt this was God's cue that another assignment awaited me. However, saying goodbye was painful, especially as I had been intimately involved in the interwoven ministries and business of the church, the bookstore, crisis counseling center and the publishing company. I loved my boss and pastor as a spiritual father. He was powerful in his prophetic anointing and generous toward the hurting. He had been so good to us. I gleaned so much from him about ministry and business. I wrote a tear-stained letter of departure and felt like I had cut off my right arm. Leaving the familiar and embracing the unknown is rarely easy. *Pastor, I bless you for your input into my life and generosity over the years. You were a spiritual father in many ways.*

We transitioned to a small independent church where Shirley and I oversaw the "home groups." I completed a "lesson plan" for the groups each week. Our home group grew in numbers and vitality over the next two years. God provided the "balm of Gilead" to heal our hurting hearts. *"Is there no balm in Gilead, is there no physician there?"* (Jeremiah 8:22a, NKJV). *"He has sent Me to heal the broken-hearted…"* (Luke 4:18b, NKJV).

Savage Release

In-laws of the tragically deceased Sherry Lee, the former crisis pregnancy client, heard that the Crisis Pregnancy Center had closed and contacted me. They knew that I had been a Christian school principal and put me in touch with a church in Maryland that was looking for a school principal. I made contact, and I was invited to an interview.

The interview, which included a sermon, went well. I was offered the position. The income was meager but included partial use of a church house. (The basement was used for youth meetings.) Details of the medical insurance were to follow.

To celebrate our upcoming move, we splurged our few savings on a trip to Disney in Florida. Shirley's persistence paid off, and we secured "cheap" air tickets and a special hotel rate of $29.95 per night (in 1995)! Our youngest son's highlight was chasing the multi-colored lizards outside the hotel. Our wonderful sons were so understanding of our financial splurge and sacrifice and never asked for extra treats like most kids. *Sons, you are and were a great blessing to us. Thank you. We wanted to give you so much more.* "But godliness with contentment is great gain" (1 Timothy 6:6, NIV). We returned from Orlando to Shippensburg ready to begin the next chapter in our lives: a move to Maryland.

Shirley was uneasy about the move but supported her hubby. We packed and loaded a long horse trailer. Whew! Then I headed to Maryland with a teen boy to help me offload. This was a trip in faith since we had not heard a response to our mailed request for full medical coverage. We arrived in Maryland and were directed to our "new" home where the teen and I unloaded the trailer. It was then that the pastor arrived, his eyes *fiercely* aflame.

"I received your letter and think it is downright disgraceful that you are demanding full medical coverage. If I had known this, I would not have offered you the job!" the pastor exploded, his face beet red.

I replied calmly to the pastor and explained that there was a need for unity for any arrangement to work. We mutually agreed to disagree. I called Shirley. She gasped audibly with relief and joy since she did not have the inner release to move. The teen and I reloaded the trailer, carting boxes up from the basement where they had been stored. We were exhausted.

The first thing I did upon returning to Shippensburg was to yank out the "For Sale" sign planted in our yard by a local realtor. I still had no work, but peace returned to the Ratcliffe residence. Shirley's face beamed! God would take care of us.

I received a phone call from the Maryland church pastor a few days later begging me to come back. He apologized profusely. I told him if he was truly sorry, he would compensate us for our efforts and expenses in moving. He surprisingly sent $300 in the mail. *Pastor, we forgive and release you, but we're not coming to Maryland. We pray God's blessings over you and your church. "For if you forgive other people when they sin against you, your heavenly Father will also forgive you. But if you do not forgive others their sins, your Father will not forgive your sins"* (Matthew 6:14–15, NIV).

Substitute Teaching

Shirley and I did not know our next step, but we trusted God's peace and that He would provide. *"Trust in the Lord with all your heart, and lean not on your own understanding; in all your ways acknowledge Him, and He shall direct your paths"* (Proverbs 3:5-6, NKJV).

Although I had a master's degree in education, full-time teaching positions in Pennsylvania were difficult to come by. I decided to pursue a state school administrator's certification through Shippensburg University in the evenings in the hopes of gaining a public school administrator's position. I did not want to return to the uncertainty of Christian school administration.

Over the next several weeks, I was registered for substitute teaching in eight area school districts, including two private Christian schools. Sometimes I would receive up to seven early morning phone calls for substitute teaching. The pay was minimal, but the Lord used it to supply our needs. I viewed substitute teaching as my "new" ministry while waiting on the Lord to reveal further direction.

A few incidents come to mind. One was a high school classroom where students were rowdy. I politely but firmly asked the students to quietly get on with their work. One girl, about sixteen years of age, was quite belligerent and refused to settle down. I slowly walked near her desk. My eyes fell on her forearms. They had multiple slashes from what looked like suicide attempts. My heart filled with compassion and my approach softened toward her. I asked if there was anything I could do to help her. She seemed somewhat taken aback at the softer "discipline" approach and settled down after that.

On another occasion, I needed to take class attendance. Unable to locate the class attendance list, I looked in the teacher's desk center drawer. I found the list and a handgun. Why would a teacher have a handgun? I quickly called the principal, who asked me (the substitute teacher) what she should do. I told her the weapon needed to be removed immediately in a concealed manner using rubber gloves to avoid adding prints. She should then contact the police. She arrived quickly and removed the handgun into a brown paper bag. The students were unaware of what was happening.

On one further occasion, I was in an upper elementary class. The class took a while to settle down. I maintained a friendly but firm demeanor throughout the day. One student asked if I would be coming back the next day. I said I would. He then told me blankly that he would bring a gun to school the following day. I took this as a direct threat and relayed the situation to the principal. The student was given a three-day suspension.

One time I was shadowing a school principal in an area school as part of my state administrator's certification. A teacher reported that a kindergarten student had brought a play gun to school. The student was given an immediate ten-day suspension. I thought this was harsh at the time but understand the need for zero tolerance of "weapons" on a school campus.

I completed the year-long administrator's course with top marks (maintaining my 4.0 GPA) and made inquiries for possible administrator positions. I interviewed for one position in Philadelphia. I was one of over thirty applicants. After another year of "no bites," I began praying about a return to Christian school administration.

Prayer and Fasting

My experience to date in America had been tumultuous with serious ramifications for my family and me. It seemed that Christian schools or crisis counseling could not afford to pay a living wage. Still, we were thankful for the Lord's provision. We lived by faith and trusted Jesus to provide all our needs. We still do.

I often reflected on Matthew 9:37: "*Then He said to His disciples, 'The harvest truly is plentiful, but the laborers are few'*" (NKJV). I wondered if this was because the laborers received little compensation. Regardless, we had seen the Lord's provision and guidance. "*His divine power has given us everything we need for a godly life through our knowledge of him who called us by his own glory and goodness*" (2 Peter 1:3, NIV).

I also found that school boards consisted of almost anyone willing to serve. The boards I had experienced to date had some wonderful people, but they were mostly unfamiliar with how to run a Christian school and had little knowledge of the philosophy of Christian school education or of educational theory and practice. Their main strength was life experience. Their "modus operandi" was generally top-down and autocratic. The same was true for church ministry and crisis counseling. Decisions made by these beautiful servants of God impacted lives, including mine and my family's, often negatively. It was against this backdrop that I set aside six days of prayer and fasting to see if God wanted me back in Christian school administration.

At the end of six days, I sensed God's peace and decided to "cast my net on the other side of the boat." "*And He said to them, 'Cast the net on the right side of the boat, and you will find some.' So they cast, and now they were not able to draw it in because of the multitude of fish"* (John 21:6, NKJV).

Christian School Administration Job Search

I interviewed for the administrator's position at a PreK-12 grade school of over 400 students in Florida's Nature Coast. Several interviews later I was offered the position. The offer was better than expected (though still significantly lower than counterparts in public school education). I agreed to "unofficially" start in April before the end of the school year so I could become better acquainted with the school and its challenges. The school had been "board run" for eighteen months as there had been no administrator.

I flew back to Pennsylvania and spent the next couple of weeks helping to ready our home for sale. Shirley was left with the bulk of the preparation, including finding a buyer for our home. Soon I flew back to Florida.

The board chairman at the Florida school found a spacious apartment above a garage several miles out in the country from the school. A local lawyer owned the apartment. *Thank you, James and Sheila, for allowing me to stay in your apartment rent-free for over a month.*

Christian School in Florida (School A)

My first day at the school was a Kindergarten Awards ceremony in the gym-chapel building. There was a large stage at one end of the building. As I observed the ceremony, I noticed smoke pouring from the top of one closed stage curtain. From the audience chatter, it seemed apparent that others noticed, too, but nobody did anything. As the school's newest (unofficial) leader, I jumped into action and "took the bull by the horns." I quickly escorted the children off the stage and went backstage to investigate. A few parents joined me. We located the issue: a stage light in contact with the top of the curtain had caused it to begin smoldering. Within minutes, we had a ladder and removed the curtain and bulb. All was now safe. *Thank You, Jesus.*

One day I received a phone call from Shirley. Our home had been sold. *Thank You, Jesus!* This was indeed an answer to prayer. A big answer!

I flew back to Pennsylvania at the end of the school year in early June. Shirley and I continued to pack, then we secured two large moving vehicles (U-Hauls) plus a driver for the long haul to Florida. The driver was a dynamic Christian teacher in a public high school. His wife, Denise, was a prolific children's author. They had several children and attended our weekly homegroup Bible study. I was the other driver. Tim and Tom came with us. The plan was for Shirley to stay with a friend in Pennsylvania and fly down a few days later. This was a well-deserved respite for the hard work she had done and for the work still ahead.

The boys and I stayed in the garage apartment and were joined by Shirley a few days later. The apartment owner and his wife had adopted several children, including one young boy named David and a girl named Sue. Years later, my younger son Tom went kayaking with David and Sue and met Sue's friend Jerrica. Tom and Jerrica later married and had four children. I share this detail to show how God orchestrates every detail of our lives. "*I will instruct thee and teach thee in the way which thou shalt go: I will guide thee with mine eye*" (Psalm 32:8, KJV).

Shortly afterward we moved into a trailer home on ten acres near the Christian school. It had a large swimming pool and included a diving board. This had previously been the location of camping grounds. God had moved us from Pennsylvania to Florida. We now had a new school, new family friends in the making, and new hope. *Thank You, Jesus!* He had delivered us from another difficult situation. "*I will praise the name of God with song and magnify Him with thanksgiving*" (Psalm 69:30, AMP).

God had made a way of escape yet again. We were still flying *above the storms*. Florida's warmer weather was welcoming, until we saw signs of fast-moving circular storms....

Shirley's Reflections

For me, moving to Florida was difficult. It was one of my most challenging moves, besides moving to America. I made some wonderful friends in Pennsylvania, and it took me about a year to adjust. I missed my friends and church passionately. Pennsylvania life had been good for us.

Our children were able to do all their elementary years at Cumberland Valley Christian School. Tom started in kindergarten, and Tim started in Grade 1. They were also immersed in softball and soccer. We were very active in our new church for our last two years in Pennsylvania.

CHAPTER 13
Florida Early Days
(1997-2002)

Crisis Faced: School A, School B – A Tale of Two Schools
Crisis: Grief – Job Bereavements
Storm: Tropical Cyclone – Rotating Storm

First Days

Florida's hurricane season lasts from May to November. Sometimes tornadoes spawn from inclement weather. My first official school day as PreK-12 grade administrator (and elementary principal) at the Christian school in Florida (or School A), was eventful. Inclement weather had rolled in out of the blue, and we were under a tornado watch. All students and staff assumed the crouched tornado positions in the main block building with sturdy school halls. Thirty minutes later, the watch ended, and school resumed as "normal." We later discovered that fifteen tornados had touched down in our county; one of them was just a mile from our school.

After this incident, one teacher quipped, "We never had this happen before. Now you are here." The remark was meant as a joke of sorts, but I could tell they had their suspicions.

Sons

Our sons did well academically and acquitted themselves well in soccer and basketball. They also both earned the Christian Character of the Year Award, of which Shirley and I were most proud. Beyond that, they had their share of bullying, particularly Tom. It was not easy being the school administrator's son, but in my eyes, they were stars who always held their composure. *So proud of you, sons of the Most High!*

Parents

Parents made appointments to see me about their children. Sometimes parents were upset. I took time to listen and pray with them. Usually these meetings went well, causing my secretary to quip once, "Parents go into your office mad but leave smiling." I took this as a compliment. Sometimes new parents visited and were unaware of what a Christian school was. I explained the vision and invited them to receive Christ. I found most parents to be very open to receiving prayer.

A couple of notable parent incidents come to mind.

One was a father who wanted information on his children's whereabouts. His ex-wife had custody of the children, and the school could not release this information. Consequently, the front staff directed him to my office. He stormed in. He was not a happy camper. He demanded to know the whereabouts of his children and glared threateningly. I wondered whether he was "packing." Three hours later, he left. He had gone from boiling over the top to simmering.

On Sunday morning, I saw him at church. I was shocked. I reflected on another parent who was equally challenging and was also a member of my church. How come the difficult parents were in my church? I've never been able to figure that out. One thing I do know is we all need Jesus!

Another parent threatened to blow up the school. It did not help that she was related to an influential parent, a lawyer, who had been very helpful to our school. I recommended decisive steps to the school board, and the parent was prohibited from accessing the school's premises.

Chapels

The school was nondenominational and evangelistic. As the school leader, I honored this posture and encouraged others to do the same. No speaking in tongues! One thing I would not compromise on, however, was allowing the Holy Spirit to move in chapel services. On a couple of occasions, students were so enraptured with the presence of the Lord that the chapel ran overtime. One chapel was three hours long. The atmosphere was electric with the presence of God. Students were weeping in repentance. It was hard to bring such a God encounter to a close. Many students were hungry to experience Jesus.

Unfortunately, certain school staff opposed the chapel services and initiated efforts to oust me from the school. What happened to the Christian family we were supposed to be? "*And 'a man's enemies will be those of his own household'*" (Matthew 10:36, NKJV).

Prayer Answered

Shirley and I had been praying about returning to Africa to see our family. Apart from an emergency trip to see my ailing father years before, we had only returned to Africa once as a complete family and once with just Shirley and the boys. Now that I was the lead administrator in a midsize Christian school, there would be little time to return to Africa. But God answered our prayer in the most unusual way.

Despite moving the school to "higher ground" academically and spiritually and helping the school to become debt-free, all was not well. Not everybody embraced the changes.

I was summoned to a meeting in early November 1999. Students were out of school for a holiday. I was told I was relieved of my position. I asked what the reason was but nothing substantive was given. No warning. No game plan for improvement. No explanation. Nothing. It seemed that a secular, corporate America mindset had influenced proceedings at the Christian school. Embracing the Holy Spirit in chapels and openly evangelizing prospective parents seemed not to be priorities.

This was a day in infamy for me. I had worked hard and given my utmost to see the school move to "higher ground." School board members who had appeared to coalesce around my leadership had suddenly turned. Inviting an administrator to resign in the middle of the year without cause was devastating. Who hired new administrators in midyear?

Massive disappointment aside, this was also a day of rejoicing. God had answered our prayers. Now we could go back to Africa and visit our loved ones…unentangled! Yes!

Amazingly, an administrator of a large Christian school in the Tampa Bay area heard of my situation and promised to discuss hiring possibilities with the board.

Y2K and Africa

This was another case of seeking the "opportunity" in the "crisis." I now had the time to return to Africa. Yet the infamous Y2K was looming. The world was in turmoil, and no one knew if computers would crash—and the world's computer-dependent systems with them. Would we ever see our family again?

Shirley's parents, my mother, a sister and one brother lived in Zimbabwe. My youngest brother lived in the UK. Shirley had a sister in Bulawayo and one in South Africa. Suddenly, and completely out of the blue, we now had time to visit family in Africa. But what about finances?

We researched tickets and found relatively inexpensive round-trip tickets to South Africa's O.R. Tambo International Airport (formerly Jan Smuts' International). *Thank You, Jesus!*

We booked a bus to Bulawayo, Zimbabwe, and stayed with Shirley's parents for an early Christmas.

Victoria Falls

Shirley's younger sister and brother-in-law kindly lent us a pickup truck with a canopy plus a caravan. This enabled us to travel several hundred miles to the Victoria Falls, one of the seven wonders of the world, on the northwestern border with Zambia. The Falls are about one mile wide and 350 feet high. The hundreds of tons of water cascading over the precipice create a mist cloud that the locals call Mosi O Tonya, the "Smoke that Thunders." This was the first (and last) time Tim and Tom saw the spectacular Falls—complete with brilliant rainbows.

We lodged at a caravan park not far from the Falls. Several other campers were present. Early one morning we heard a shriek. A lady in a nearby rondavel (traditional round dwelling) was hollering loudly. We soon discovered that she had awakened to the feel of "fingers" raking through her hair. Apparently a baboon had found her hair attractive. She had left a door ajar for fresh air, which allowed the baboon access.

Baboons and monkeys were prolific at the park. Most seemed used to humans. However, having been raised in Zimbabwe, I knew that baboons could rip the fiercest dog apart. One could only imagine what an angry baboon could do to a human.

Memory Lane

We returned to Shirley's hometown and then embarked on a round trip to my mother's on the other side of the country. En route, we visited my childhood home in the flatlands of the Somabula bush. The boys and Shirley could not understand what I found in this place. Little did they realize the childhood joys of the African bush and riding the African neighbors' donkeys through the tall African bushveld.

We visited my childhood school and were exiting the isolated Somabula railway "village" when cattle completely blockaded the narrow "strip" road. A local white African rancher saw us and inquired about our journey. He was enthralled to hear that I had once been a student at Somabula Primary (elementary) and that I knew his friends the Hepalts, who were local ranchers. He excitedly exclaimed that they were home and would be excited to see us.

A mile later down a winding dirt road, we arrived at the Hepalts' ranch house. We quickly caught up on the news. I learned from Mr. and Mrs. Hepalt that their daughter Donna, who had been in my class, was now a pharmacist in South Africa. I also learned that a few years after my family had left Somabula, guerrilla-terrorists had murdered five white farmers when they attacked the local farmers' country club. This was where I learned to play tennis. So sad. This was the same club where years before, as a child in 1967, I had asked the visiting prime minister, Ian Smith, and his wife, Janet Smith, to "pose" for a photograph.

After a good "cuppa" and some cookies, it was time to leave. Mr. Hepalt generously blessed Tim (fifteen) and Tom (thirteen) with a real hippo tooth and a giant ostrich egg each. What a treat! The boys beamed.

We made another stop a few hours later at a school where I had been the principal and Shirley had been the teacher. So many memories. We also had a late afternoon meal with my not-so-"old" school secretary, Patsy Oosthuizen. *Thank you, Patsy, for your generosity and kindness that day and all the days when I was the principal at Umniati (now Munyati)*

Primary School. You were an amazing secretary and confidante. Shirley and I enjoyed our tennis times with you and your family.

We continued our trip to my mother's home hundreds of miles away but stopped at friends' for the night in Harare—David Stevenson and his wife. David was a lawyer and the District Commissioner (DC) who presided over the legal aspects of our marriage in 1981.

The African sun had already set, and I remember seeing a giant golden moon balanced delicately on the horizon as though perched deftly on the road ahead of us.

Mutare Reunion

After visiting our friends, we continued to mountainous Mutare for several more hours' drive. Cresting Christmas Pass was breathtaking and reminded us of what pioneers not so long ago experienced as their wagons crested the mountain to see an expansive wooded valley below. How awe-inspiring! We soon arrived at the Lodge, the home my parents had originally bought in Mutare and later sold to my brother Brian and his wife, Natalie, who developed it into a bed and breakfast.

My brother Liam and his family, my sister, Mary, and her family, my brother Brian and his family, my mother and her new husband, Alistair, and our family, enjoyed a few days of respite and celebrated a wonderful Christmas together. Ahh. It was wonderful and refreshing to be back in Africa, back home breathing fresh African mountain air.

Soon Shirley, Tim, Tom and I returned to Shirley's parents in Bulawayo.

Answered Prayer

About halfway through our six-week trip back to Africa, I received an email from the Christian school administrator in Tampa. The school board was very interested in hiring me. I was offered the newly created position of Elementary/Middle Principal with a start date of January 31, 2000. *Thank You, Jesus!* How perfect!

Schools do not typically create positions for new and unknown principal-administrators midway through a school year! But God is faithful to answer prayer. "*And this is the confidence that we have toward him, that if we ask anything according to his will he hears us. And if we know that he hears us in whatever we ask, we know that we have the requests that we have asked of him*" (1 John 5:14–15, ESV). Shirley and I were overjoyed to receive the good news. Our hearts rejoiced. "*Lord, our Lord, how majestic is your name in all the earth*" (Psalm 8:9, NIV). God again took care of us despite our being on a different continent. *Thank You, Jesus!* Soon we were winging our way back to Florida in the United States.

Christian School in Tampa Bay (School B)

The first morning's drive to the Christian school in Tampa Bay from our home should have taken just over an hour. Instead, a vehicle accident ahead of us created a massive traffic backlog that resulted in my being two hours late. Fortunately, this was not the norm.

I settled in quickly at the school and forged some wonderful relationships. The leadership team was comprised of the lead administrator, the high school principal and me. We had a weekly meeting that started with prayer and addressed school issues. I was quickly enlisted to share in the Wednesday evening church meals held in the cafeteria. Occasionally I would present a gospel message.

I was required to be a church member since I was part of the school leadership. This meant waking up a little earlier and ensuring that Tim, Tom and I were ready for the morning commute to Tampa. I played the guitar in the church band. Tim played the trumpet and Tom played the trombone. The boys wanted to return to our "regular" church near our home but participated all the same.

Doctoral Acceptance

Before leaving the first Christian school, School A, I had applied to the doctoral program at Oral Roberts University in Tulsa, Oklahoma. This was a step of faith. The Lord had dropped the word *doctorate* in my spirit several years earlier in Pennsylvania. This was where I completed my master's degree in education. The blend of faith, healing, prayer and strong academics was an excellent match for my career and ministry pursuits.

I visited ORU and closely examined all aspects of the Doctorate in Educational Leadership program. I sensed God's hand of approval and believed I could "climb this mountain." I submitted my application.

A few months later at the Tampa Christian school (School B), I received the electrifying news that I had been accepted into the program. This was a step of faith. I trusted the Lord for His provision. I shared the good news with the lead administrator. A short while later she informed me that the school board would cover tuition costs. I was elated. God was meeting my needs. *Thank You, Jesus!* "*Carry each other's burdens, and in this way you will fulfill the law of Christ*" (Galatians 6:2, NIV).

Stabbing

A back-to-school evening was planned for parents the week before school started. Parents attended with their children. The church auditorium was packed to capacity. I was seated with the leadership team at the front of the church. We were just about to begin the program when suddenly Tim, our fifteen-year-old son, dashed to me at the front.

"Dad, a man has been stabbed. He's bleeding badly."

I quickly excused myself and hurried to the back of the church and through the streetside foyer entrance. A man lay bleeding profusely from chest wounds. I knelt by his side and spoke briefly to him. He told me that he'd been accosted and stabbed by area gang members.

Tim took charge of the bystanders. "You, call 911," he directed a man he later found out was the high school principal. He asked others to stand back so the man had air to breathe and some space.

"Sir, the ambulance is coming. Are you at peace with Jesus?" I asked. The man nodded slightly. I asked if I could pray for him. He agreed. "Father, bring Your peace and healing to this man. Please help the bleeding to stop. In Jesus' name, I pray."

The ambulance arrived quite quickly, and capable personnel loaded him onto a gurney and then in through the open back door of the ambulance.

I returned to the front of the church and joined the leadership team. We discussed our joint approach moving forward. I was "volunteered" to address the audience and tell them what they needed to know. We decided to share only the facts, not the unconfirmed details in order not to "spook" the audience. However, we needed to share sufficient information to ensure we were doing the right thing as a school and not opening ourselves to legal pursuits.

"Ladies and gentlemen, students," I began, "welcome to our Parent Evening. It is wonderful to see you all here. Please be mindful of your surroundings when you leave. We had one parent who had an incident and is now safely in an ambulance on his way to the hospital. We value your prayers for this parent." End of communiqué. Whew! There was no mass exodus from the building. No stampede. Sigh of relief.

The school received an update on the situation a few days later. The man was the father of a student at the school; however, he was in a custody dispute with his estranged wife. The stab wounds had been self-inflicted to shock his wife into sympathy in the hopes of restoring the family. Tim's empathy for the wounded man was eviscerated instantly. He'd been hoodwinked, and so had I. How sad it is when relationships are frayed so irreparably. *"Though one may be overpowered, two can defend themselves. A cord of three strands is not quickly broken"* (Ecclesiastes 4:12, NIV).

Tim and Tom

The boys traveled with me in the new 2000-2001 school year, which meant early mornings and sometimes late evenings. I would rise at 5:00 a.m. or earlier and at about 5:30 a.m. announce my presence to the boys by crooning a catchy upbeat jingle with the aid of my British-made ukulele banjo. They often covered their ears, but the song did the trick. The words to this extemporaneous song went something like this: "It's time, it's time, it's time to go to school..." repeated ad nauseum until the boys roused from slumber.

Forgive me, my sons. I know you were tired. Thank you for playing along with my attempts to get you up early. Now the roosters and grandkiddos wake you up early!

The boys spent some long days at school, especially when playing on the soccer team. They were both accomplished soccer players. In one game, Tim booted the ball from the center line into the back of the goal net. *Way to go, Tim!*

Tim and Tom were invited to spend half-school days at one teacher's home. Her son attended high school, too. They enjoyed many hours waterskiing on the lake at the back of their home and hanging out with their friend and his family. The teacher knew what teenage boys loved— food—and cooked them scrumptious meals.

Tom approached me after the first year. He wanted to transition to a local high school much closer to our home. The days were long, and he needed more sleep. He also felt that many students knew how to speak "Christianese" while living a lifestyle that dishonored the Lord.

Shirley and I discussed Tom's plea and prayed fervently. I was a passionately strong advocate of Christian school education but could see Tom's level of joy plummeting. Shirley and I agreed to let Tom go to a local public school. I remember driving home one day by myself during the summer and weeping almost uncontrollably the entire trip. I could feel my son's pain. I had to release him into God's hands.

I tried never to miss Timothy's games, including the athletic events where he threw the discus and shot put and ran track. *Way to go, son!* (Tom played on the local public school varsity soccer team and had an intuitive read on the game. Shirley and I attended home games when possible. He was also a breakthrough cross-country runner. *Way to go, Tom!*)

Tim was interested in being an EMT and was taking EMT classes while still at school. I headed up the paperwork with the local state college and liaised with the Tampa church school to allow Timothy to be dual-enrolled. Hopefully, other budding EMT students gleaned from this benefit, too.

I worked on my doctoral studies once the school day was over and while waiting for Tim to finish up sports practice. A retired statistics professor helped me to decide on a stepwise multiple regression analysis for my quantitative-based study. The study investigated the correlation between effective schools and student achievement.

Emergency Call: Mom

One day I received a call from my "baby" brother, Liam, the highly qualified physician and researcher (and later businessman). He worked in England at the time. "Mom is in a coma in Johannesburg, South Africa. If you want to see her alive, you will need to go soon. She had failed open-heart surgery that resulted in internal bleeding. There's nothing more doctors can do."

The school graciously granted me time off in May 2001. I flew to Johannesburg, South Africa, and stayed in a hotel near Mill Park Hospital. Liam had made the accommodation arrangements and generously paid for the hotel. Our sister, Mary, also stayed at the hotel. She had flown in from South Africa with her daughter Bridget. Brian (Kiey), our brother who still lived in Zimbabwe, was due to arrive the following week.

It was hard to see Mom in a hospital bed in a coma with tubes up her nose, hooked up to an IV, and lips parched. I gently dabbed her lips with cool water using a cotton ball. One day I walked several miles to a church and purchased a cassette with gentle Gaelic hymns and songs. I taped over one song and added a simple gospel message. I was concerned for my mother's eternal soul. She had raised us in the "fear of the Lord" and clearly believed in God, but I never knew if she had a personal "born again" relationship with Jesus, if she knew Him as her Lord and Savior.

Another day we siblings toured a local bookstore. I found a music corner where you could listen to songs and selected an Irish song that caught my attention. The song was a ballad about a son who'd wandered off to seek his fortune elsewhere. His mother sat by the kitchen window watching daily for her beloved son's return. The kettle was boiling for a cup of tea. Her son never returned home.

I was instantly carried away by the mournful ballad and for the first time realized the excruciating pain my mother must have suffered when I, her eldest, emigrated to America, never to return permanently. I wept alone, uncontrollably. Mom was in a coma. I felt like I was the son in the song.

I extended my stay to three weeks. My school back in Tampa was understanding and gracious.

Doctors had practically given up on Mom. The first triple bypass resulted in internal bleeding. The second operation was too much for Mom and triggered a coma. Doctors could not communicate with her, but I thought I'd try.

Mom and us siblings used to play a game called "Twenty Questions." The "it" person thought of something, and others had up to twenty "yes" or "no" questions to figure out the answer. I told Mom to squeeze my hand once for "yes" and twice for "no," and I would try and answer a question.

"Is it living?" One slight squeeze (yes).

"Is it in Africa?" Another slight squeeze.

"Is it human?" Slight squeeze.

"Do you know this person?" Two slight squeezes.

The "game" continued until we got to the point where Mom wanted to know the name of the person in a bed near her. Not bad for a comatose person. Mom's brain was still active even if she could not open her eyes and speak or move her body. Mom always was an enigma.

One difficult medical decision I deferred to my sister, Mary (a nurse), and brother Liam (a physician) was whether Mom should have a tracheotomy to help her breathe better. They opted for the procedure, which was scheduled for a few days later.

On the Thursday before Mother's Day of 2001, I bade farewell to my dear mother. My heart was heavy. We didn't know whether she would be in a coma for six months or just a few more days, or whether she'd ever recover. I wished my mother a "Happy Mother's Day" and bought her colorful flowers. One nurse commented on seeing the siblings around Mom's bed. "You must love your mother very much to have traveled from all around the world to be at her bedside." We literally lived in countries on four different continents: England (Liam), Zimbabwe (Brian), New Zealand (Mary) and America (me, Martin). My mother had stressed to us growing up that we were to "spread our wings and fly." I don't think she meant for us to fly that far.

I had a heavy and despondent heart on the flight back from Johannesburg, South Africa, to Florida, USA. I so desperately wanted a shoulder to cry on, literally. I knew that my father had died after I left him in 1991. Now Mom was facing a life-and-death situation, and the prognosis was grim. I prayed and silently wept warm, copious tears. I could sense God's presence even through the tears. "*Jesus wept*" (John 11:35, KJV). "*For we do not have a high priest who is unable to empathize with our weaknesses* [infirmities], *but we have one who has been tempted in every way, just as we are—yet he did not sin*" (Hebrews 4:15, NIV).

Return to Work

I returned home on Friday. On Sunday, I received an unwelcome call. Mom passed away on Mother's Day. The medical complications proved to be too much. I wept. Again. Losing a loved one is hard. Very hard.

On Monday, I returned to the hustle and bustle of the last few weeks of school. I led the elementary chapels on occasion and composed little songs for the children. One song was titled, "Are You a Freezer Pop?" Another was about Isaac Newton. Still another was titled, "Fly Like an Eagle." All the songs had a message and the gospel and were played in an upbeat manner on the guitar.

Shrinking Lake

I was called into the lead administrator's office at the end of the school year. She looked forlorn and said, "I regret to inform you that our school enrollment has dropped, and we will not be able to offer you the Elementary/Middle School Principal position for next year. However, we have a teacher's position and hope that you will consider this." She was truly sorry. However, surviving on a lower salary while driving so long to school daily was out of the question.

The Lord had given me a dream about two weeks prior. I saw a lake with a boat. The lake was shrinking, and the boat was dragged out of the water. I knew ahead of time that the Lord was warning me that my time was up at the Christian school in Tampa Bay. Nevertheless, it was still sad. I had grown to love and appreciate the lead administrator. She was an amazing school leader who led with integrity, gentleness and professionalism, qualities that I admire and have tried to emulate.

God receives all the glory for His deliverance and power enabling us to soar once again *above the storms*. It was hard to imagine that storms driven by strong winds were just beyond the magnificent Florida horizon....

Shirley's Reflections

Even though losing the job at our first school in Florida was extremely painful, it opened the door for us to travel back to Zimbabwe for

Christmas. My children had only met their grandparents and extended family once, and that was when they were very young. Now they were teenagers. They were able to experience and enjoy the African people and the amazing wildlife. Great memories were forged. *"And we know that for those who love God all things work together for good, for those who are called according to his purpose"* (Romans 8:28, ESV).

CHAPTER 14

Florida Days

(2002-2013)

Crisis Faced: Doctorate – Finish the Race
Crisis: Educational – Up Is Down
Storm: Derecho – Organized Thunderstorms, Strong Winds

Administrator to Teacher

I loved serving as a Christian school principal and administrator. I loved the students, staff and parents. I wanted to remain in school administration, but I was learning painfully that our ways are not always His ways. "*For as the heavens are higher than the earth, so are My ways higher than your ways, and My thoughts than your thoughts*" (Isaiah 55:9, NKJV).

Searching for another school administrator's position would have meant leaving our home and church and uprooting the boys. Tim was entering his senior year at the Christian school in Tampa Bay, and Tom was entering his sophomore year at the local public high school. I was working hard on my doctorate but had a way to go. After talking it out with Shirley and praying, we felt the best option was for me to serve in public education.

I applied for several positions and was eventually offered a fifth-grade teacher's position teaching all subject areas at Floyd Elementary School in Hernando County, Florida. I quickly adjusted back to classroom teaching. After all, I initially trained as an elementary teacher and enjoyed the challenges of teaching multiple subject areas. I was a hands-on teacher and involved students in projects.

Creative Science Teaching

One project almost got me in trouble with one bus driver. He did not allow *live animals* on his bus. I had collected dozens of tadpoles from pools of water in the open roadside grass drain at our home. I decided that each student could have his or her own tadpole and keep it in a jar. (We also had tadpoles in a fish tank.) The students took the tadpoles home over the weekends and brought them back to school on Mondays. This allowed for daily observations and recording of data. We undertook a project as a class to determine if the oxygen levels in the water had an impact on tadpole development. Students were enthusiastically engaged in the project and demonstrated science learning gains.

Another science project was based on a question I had asked students at all levels since arriving in America many years before. I asked this question in part so that students would use data to correct deeply held assumptions. "What color is blood *inside* the body?" An initial survey showed results consistent with my informal survey of this question to students of all ages and several states across America. About two-thirds claimed that blood was blue inside the body but turned red when it encountered the oxygen in the air outside the body. About one-third of the fifth-grade students said blood was red inside the body. A small percentage claimed an assortment of other colors.

I deftly guided the students through the key steps of scientific inquiry, including a research question, data collection, data analysis, the experiment and results, and conclusion, and helped them to form a hypothesis (and null hypothesis). I provided careful instruction and practical examples showing that a straw's color does not change the color of the fluid in the straw. This helped some students to see that just because veins appear green or blue does not mean that the blood is green or blue. I also showed students a syringe without a needle and explained that all air is expelled from the syringe before drawing blood. Blood drawn by a phlebotomist or nurse is dark red, but it is still red—not blue or purple or green or any other color!

The students responded positively to the science project and practically one hundred percent said blood was red inside the body in the post survey. Whew! *American Heart Association, I think you have your work cut out for you.*

Doctorate in Educational Leadership

I had started my doctorate while at the Tampa Christian school and had been working on it for just over two years. I continued to work on it in the early morning hours, evenings and weekends. I found that nobody was jostling for our lone desktop computer at 3:30 in the morning. Plus, I felt I was able to think clearly after doing my quiet time and prayer time.

Eventually it became time to sit for comprehensive written and oral exams. I studied intensively for about four months, putting in over 600 hours of study time. I was amazed at my brain's ability to absorb and digest vast quantities of critical information and to make the necessary connections. I was a "plodder" who had to work hard to reach major accomplishments.

The efforts paid off and I advanced to the dissertation phase. *Thank You, Jesus. "…All things are possible to him who believes"* (Mark 9:23, NKJV). I found that prayer and intense preparation are key, along with strong support from one's dear spouse and family!

My first (almost) dissertation chair died suddenly. The next chair quit after a couple of years, as he had other responsibilities. My "third" chair was a Godsend but insisted that I redo my dissertation to make it more research-based. This was earth-shattering news as I had worked long and hard and hoped to graduate soon. I did not relish the thought of going through the agonizing dissertation permission hoops, which were detailed and time-consuming, again. However, I understood their necessity. I prayerfully decided to calmly respond and believed that such a travesty had happened in some way for my good. *"And we know that in all things God works for the good of those who love him, who have been called according to his purpose"* (Romans 8:28, NIV). I purposefully chose to emulate Esther in the Bible: *"…And who knows but that you have come to your royal position **for such a time as this?**"* (Esther 4:14, NIV, emphasis added).

The dissertation phase was strenuous and seemed like it would never end. I had told Shirley before we started that the usual five-year doctoral process would probably take me four years since I had transferred credits earned from my principal's certification in Pennsylvania. Alas, the years rolled by. Shirley often asked, "Are you nearly done yet?" She wanted life to revert to normal, whatever *normal* was.

Finally, it was time to defend my dissertation. The major hurdle was having everything aligned with the university's strict standards. I made three attempts to arrange to defend my dissertation. However, minor formatting and APA writing glitches still needed to be resolved. I even received a phone call the night before flying to Tulsa to defend my dissertation. There was *still* minutia to take care of. My defense was delayed. Again. I was *beyond* exasperated!

Shirley and I had invited long-term friends Larry and Julianna Walker to travel down from Arkansas to Tulsa for the proposed December 2006 graduation date. However, the pressure of having to *again* clean up minuscule dissertation glitches caused me to focus on the task at hand. I completely forgot to call Larry and Juliana, who still made the trip to ORU. They were gracious enough to call me and see how I was doing. They decided to "make a mini vacation" out of the time away from ministry and booked a hotel for a couple of nights. *Larry and Juliana, thank you for your grace extended to me. So sorry I forgot to call you.* "A friend loves at all times" (Proverbs 17:17a, NIV).

Finally, a few weeks later, everything was approved, and everyone signed off on the dissertation. A mammoth feat! On to more review and defense preparation.

Dissertation Defense

I flew to Tulsa and met my chair for dinner. I learned that a massive snowstorm was moving into the area the following day. My chair was calming and reassuring. He also made me aware of potential "sand traps" with certain individuals throwing "curveball" questions to get me "off track."

I was "studied up" and "prayed up." I just needed the snowstorm to hold off.

The morning sky was azure without a hint of what was to come. I traveled sedately to the ORU campus and defense room. I was hypervigilant and super-prepared for tough defense questions. The room was packed. The presentation part of the defense went off without a hitch. Next were the questions. I maintained my composure and refused to become a statistic. God was with me. He was my defense.

The questions began and continued in rapid-fire succession. I could "smell" a curveball question coming from a senior faculty member. I answered all the questions carefully and confidently. I heeded my chair's advice.

Before I knew it, I was escorted from the defense room. Now the "committee" would decide if I was to become a doctor or return to the trenches without my Ed.D. and become an "ABD"—All But Dissertation candidate, the equivalent of "FLD," or Failed. About fifteen minutes later the conference door opened. I was escorted back into the room. The dean introduced me to the committee at large. "Ladies and gentlemen, it is my pleasure to introduce to you Dr. Martin Ratcliffe." Applause erupted. My smile could have filled the Grand Canyon. *Thank You, Jesus.* "*From the fruit of their lips people are filled with good things, and the work of their hands brings them reward*" (Proverbs 12:14, NIV). "*All hard work brings a profit, but mere talk leads only to poverty*" (Proverbs 14:23, NIV).

The promised snowstorm blanketed the area that afternoon and evening and shut down the Tulsa airport. I had to stay another night at the hotel, yet my heart was glad. With God's grace and strength, I had accomplished a lifelong goal: to become a doctor, albeit not a medical doctor.

Graduation

Graduation was scheduled for May 5, 2007. Unbeknownst to me, Shirley had contacted my brother Liam in Connecticut and my sister in New Zealand. Both flew in for the big day. Mary dressed up in a wig and tried to surprise me at the hotel room door. But I would recognize those Irish eyes anywhere. *Good try, Mary. Thank you, Mary and Liam, for your loving support throughout the years and across the miles. You rock!*

The Victory Christian Center—the location for the graduation—was practically filled. Hundreds of students were set to graduate—undergraduates, graduates and doctoral. I sat with my peers. I was one of five graduating doctoral students from over 300 students matriculating through the doctoral process. It had not been an easy climb, but God was merciful and gracious and enabled me to persevere to the finish line. *"And let us run with perseverance the race marked out for us"* (Hebrews 12:1c, NIV). I asked each of the other doctoral graduates their story. I had taken over seven years, all told, to graduate. One doctoral student had taken nine years, another nine and a half. I suddenly realized that I had taken less time than others, although it seemed like a lifetime, especially for Shirley and my sons. *Thank you, dear Shirley, Tim and Tom, for your unwavering support during my doctoral studies. I accomplished a dream, but I know that you paid heavily for it. I hope that in some way this accomplishment will inspire you to do the "impossible." "Commit to the Lord whatever you do, and he will establish your plans"* (Proverbs 16:3, NIV). *"I press toward the goal for the prize of the upward call of God in Christ Jesus"* (Philippians 3:14, NKJV).

Assistant Education Professor

One of my original goals in completing the doctorate was to be a professor at a Christian university. I hoped that Tim and Tom would have "free" (or reduced) access to higher education—a perk of their dad being employed at the university. Alas, this was not the case. Tim and Tom had graduated from high school a few years prior and entered the emergency services field as EMTs and later paramedics. Tom later became a nurse. Still later, Tim was promoted to driver engineer.

I was offered an assistant education professor position at Oklahoma Wesleyan University in Oklahoma but returned to Florida after a year. We still had our home and easily transitioned back. We trusted God for a similar position closer to home where our family was. *"A person's steps are directed by the Lord. How then can anyone understand their own way?"* (Proverbs 20:24, NIV).

I decided to call Southeastern University in Lakeland, Florida, which was a drive of about an hour and twenty minutes from home. I had inquired earlier about an education professor's position there but was told to apply for an adjunct position. An adjunct position would not pay the bills. Dr. Bennet, the new education dean, took my call.

"Sorry, we don't have any openings right now. You can apply online for an adjunct position. Goodbye."

Dr. Bennet called me a couple of hours later. "We just had one of our professors resign. We have a position open. When can you interview?"

I was offered the position after successful interviews with the education faculty and university president Dr. Rutland. *Thank You, Jesus!*

I served at Southeastern University for four years. At first I taught undergraduate education classes and graduate research face-to-face. Later I taught online classes as well. I loved the students and would often bring my ukulele banjo to class to help create an uplifting atmosphere. The students mostly enjoyed the jingles. One student later reported that she was feeling depressed one day while driving to a school to complete a practicum. "I was driving and feeling down when that silly jingle popped into my brain. By the time I arrived at school, I was smiling."

I made several friends, including my dean, Dr. Bennett. He and I dressed in doctor's white coats and recorded a skit about "operating" on a needy patient (education). We even listed ourselves online with a company that had big-name speakers. He was called the "heart of education" (believing the best outcomes happened when we touched a student's heart), and I was called the "brain of education" (stressing the need for academic excellence). Together we made quite a duo.

"Maximus" Miracle

Shirley and I moved into an apartment next to Southeastern University to cut down on daily commutes. This allowed Shirley to work with a local hospice agency. I was able to walk to my office. We both enjoyed occasional meals at the university café and, overall, enjoyed our new life together living next to Southeastern University in Lakeland, Florida. On the evening of October 8, 2009, we received a phone call from our son Tim. "Tom has been in an accident. He is being flown by helicopter to a trauma unit." Our world stopped spinning. Tim's super calm and reassuring voice helped us to breathe. Our youngest son was alive. No need to panic. Pray!

We rushed to the trauma unit about an hour away. Tom was lying still on a gurney, his neck in a brace. We had learned from Tim that a vehicle had unlawfully crossed Tom's path on a busy highway. Tom's truck

T-boned the other vehicle. His airbag exploded and saved his life. His pickup was demolished, however. The driver of the other vehicle walked away without injury. This was her second vehicle accident in one week.

"I'm ready to meet Jesus if this is my time," Tom whispered. We could see the pain on his face. What courage in the face of danger, just like his "look-alike" movie hero, Maximus (Russell Crow), in *Gladiator*. We later discovered that Tom's neck was okay, but he had several bulging and herniated discs in his lower back. *Thank You, Jesus, for saving our son's life!*

Marriages

Tim, our eldest son, became engaged over Christmas 2008 when I had returned from Oklahoma for the Christmas break and before Shirley and I made a joint trek to Oklahoma (for the second semester). We flew back in early April for the wedding on April 4, 2009. It was a beautiful day with an outside wedding complete with horse and carriage for the beautiful bride, Carissia.

Tom was married a couple of years later in 2010 on our anniversary, April 25th, in a local country church. Jerrica wore her cowboy boots, a fitting sign of the adventurous life to come. Both brides were a gift from God and the answers to our prayers. God is so good. God answers *"the effective, fervent prayer of a righteous man* [and woman]" (James 5:16, NKJV). Our sons had indeed found virtuous brides. *"Who can find a virtuous wife? For her worth is far above rubies. The heart of her husband safely trusts her; so he will have no lack of gain"* (Proverbs 31:10–11, NKJV).

Mission Trips

I had represented the university in El Salvador at a major K-12 school convention for Latin American countries. I was well received and even composed a motivational jingle in Spanish with the help of a Spanish-speaking friend. Additionally, I spoke in breakout sessions at several education conventions in America. I also went to India on missions with my church and integrated the experiences back into my lessons. At one point during a presentation to several hundred Indian pastors and their wives in a large colorful tent, I asked who wanted prayer for healing. Then I prayed. After the prayer, I asked who had been healed. Hands shot up throughout the tent. I then sat down. Suddenly a terrific wind out of nowhere blew in like a small hurricane and threatened to rip the tent from its moorings. The large central supporting pole near the stage was lifted off its base. I quickly grabbed the microphone and commanded the wind to be calm "in Jesus' name." The wind obeyed and calmness was restored. Apparently the demonic realm was not pleased with God moving inside the tent. *"Behold, I give unto you power to tread on serpents and scorpions, and over all the power of the enemy: and nothing shall by any means hurt you. Notwithstanding in this rejoice not, that the spirits are subject unto you; but rather rejoice, because your names are written in heaven"* (Luke 10:19–20, KJV).

Kiey

I heard that my brother Brian, or Kiey, as we called him, was having tests at a clinic in his hometown of Mutare in Zimbabwe, Africa. He had returned from a shopping spree road trip to South Africa and was not feeling well. A few days later Liam (a doctor now in the USA) called me with an update. Kiey had been hospitalized, but the doctors did not know what was wrong. A few days later, Liam called with an urgent update. Brian had flown to Cape Town and was in a hospital there. Doctors had diagnosed the worst kind of leukemia. He also had contracted the flesh-eating virus, *necrotizing fasciitis*. Liam urged me to fly to South Africa as soon as possible.

I prayed and felt the Lord impressing me to fly immediately to South Africa but to go through London then to Johannesburg and onto Cape Town. This was clear enough. However, I hesitated to decide since I had to prepare for work and research airlines. I booked a day later and arrived in Cape Town at Kiey's hospital bedside three hours before he passed on April 21, 2011. Had I instantly "obeyed" the Lord, I may have had more time with my loving brother. *"Behold, to obey is better than sacrifice, and to heed than the fat of rams"* (1 Samuel 15:22b, NKJV).

We held a memorial service in Cape Town, South Africa, at a majestic mountainside park filled with flowers. A couple of days later, I transported Kiey's ashes to his beautiful hometown of Mutare in Zimbabwe some 1,500 miles or more away. I helped to officiate at the funeral and briefly presented the gospel. One pastor and friend of Kiey's explained how Kiey had attended a Bible study for the past couple of years. I had also just written a letter of appeal to Kiey a couple of weeks before to make sure everything was in order with the Lord. I believe I will see my brother again one day in heaven. *Love you, Kiey.*

News Bomb

Southeastern University represented the pinnacle of my academic and career pursuits. I had worked very hard over many years and the Lord saw fit to open a door at Southeastern University. I got along well with faculty, staff and students, made presentations to peers, and was actively involved in the fabric of the university. I had even published an education book titled *Schools That Make the Grade: What Successful Schools Do to Improve Student Achievement.* I felt I had won the respect of my peers.

Shirley and I were happy living next to the university. We attended the inexpensive yet outstanding student drama performances and other events. We enjoyed socializing and meeting new friends. Shirley worked for a local hospice agency and was "just what the doctor ordered" for the ailing elderly folk she served. *I love you, my beautiful and faithful bride!*

Tom, our younger son, continued to live in our former home now with his amazing bride, Jerrica. Shirley and I returned on weekends so we could attend church. In retrospect, we realize the importance of newlyweds having their own space. *Tom and Jerrica, we are truly sorry if you felt crowded out on weekends. Please forgive us.*

Tom and Jerrica later moved to a "new" dwelling. After two years in the apartment near the university, we moved back to our house. I resumed my daily commutes to the university.

Then came the "news bomb"! I was called into the provost's office and politely told that I had been cut (along with several other faculty) for budget reasons. They expressed regret and thanked me for my service. My world crashed!

I returned from the provost's office and was greeted outside by a colleague and friend. We sat outside the main entrance to the education building and wept together. "*Weeping may endure for a night, but joy comes in the morning*" (Psalm 30:5b, NKJV).

It is amazing how one decision can alter one's life so immediately and dramatically and with such finality. The job loss was a bitter pill to swallow, but God was *still* in control. "*In him we were also chosen, having been predestined according to the plan of him who works out everything in conformity with the purpose of his will*" (Ephesians 1:11, NIV).

I drove the fifty-five-plus miles (about ninety kilometers) home sedately after classes. I needed windshield wipers on my eyeballs to wipe the torrents of tears away. My grief was palpable and almost uncontrollable. My son Tim called and asked how everything was going. I whispered my story amidst tearful cascades. I felt like a spitfire fighter plane in World War II riddled with enemy fire limping back across the English Channel to the homeland. Beside me was a fellow fighter, my son Timothy, flying confidently and gently coaching me along the homestretch to a safe home landing. *Thank you, son, for your kindness. God used you to buoy me up on one of the lowest days of my life. And I have had many.*

I have been learning for many years to trust the Lord regardless of whether anything makes sense or not. Usually it doesn't. Change can be painful. Forced change can rip your heart apart. But if we trust Jesus in our words and actions, He will make something beautiful from our ashes. "*To console those who mourn in Zion, to give them beauty for ashes, the oil of joy for mourning, the garment of praise for the spirit of heaviness; that they may be called trees of righteousness, the planting of the Lord, that He may be glorified*" (Isaiah 61:3, NKJV). "*For His anger is but for a moment, His favor is for life; weeping may endure for a night, but joy comes in the morning*" (Psalm 30:5, NKJV).

About ten years later, I heard that the university went through another pruning, resulting in faculty members being cut and salaries frozen. In God's foreknowledge, I may have been spared this second pruning, allowing me to bloom elsewhere. *Thank You, Jesus!* "*Most assuredly, I say to you that you will weep and lament, but the world will rejoice; and you will be sorrowful, but your sorrow will be turned into joy*" (John 16:20, NKJV).

Pacemaker

Concurrent with losing my position, Shirley was facing the prospect of a pacemaker to help regulate her racing, and at other times, slow, molasses-like heartbeat. I appealed to the university through my former dean and good friend, Dr. Bennett, for a one-semester extension so the medical insurance would still be intact. The university graciously extended my tenure for one semester. I taught online classes from home and remained on the university's good medical plan. *Thank You, Jesus!*

Shirley received her first pacemaker in May of 2012. A home nurse came to remove the staples. He wasn't joking when he said he'd watched the procedure on YouTube. He had the staple remover the wrong way around. He enlarged the puncture sites while trying to wrestle out the staples. Shirley squeezed my hand in a vice grip throughout the whole ordeal and then became unresponsive. This resulted in a trip by ambulance back to the hospital for an overnight stay.

Shirley developed an infection a few weeks later after swimming with a friend. The pacemaker had to be removed, and she was on an antibiotic drip for three months. It was eventually replaced when the infection cleared in November 2012. We learned that surgeons rarely replace pacemakers because of infection; it was "a one percent chance," according to Shirley's electrophysiologist. Through it all, God was faithful, and the expensive bill was completely taken care of. *Thank You, Jesus. "The Lord is my shepherd; I shall not want. He maketh me to lie down in green pastures: he leadeth me beside the still waters. He restoreth my soul: he leadeth me in the paths of righteousness for his name's sake"* (Psalm 23:1–3, KJV).

Test of Faith

I had reached my dream job in higher Christian education. I loved being an assistant education professor. Loved the students. Loved my peers. Loved the freedom to have a cup of "free" coffee in the college cafeteria and converse with peers and students. I fit at the Christian university campus and could relate to people from diverse backgrounds. And I was accepted…that is, until the budget cuts.

I immediately embarked on an almost two-year journey to find a similar position. Anything but a return to the classroom!

One job opportunity surfaced at Zhengzhou University in China. It had an "American" track where students could graduate with American degrees. Shirley was offered a position in the attached K-5 school. We interviewed, were accepted and prepared to go to China. However, we had not heard directly from the Lord....

The weeks ebbed by. Our cases were packed. The more time passed, the more we realized we needed to sell our home. It would be difficult to rent our home while living in China, and if something went wrong, how could we attend to it? And where would the finances come from? The pay in China was dismal and more like a stipend. However, our airfares, accommodation and food would be mostly covered. Still, we were unemployed in America and needed to pay the monthly mortgage.

The realization hit us squarely between the eyes. It was all or nothing. Yes, we would obey God, if this was what *He* was asking of us. Yes, we would sell the home we loved, the home God had picked out for us years before when He answered our prayers. We had given God our "yes" years before and were not about to turn back now. Both our sons had expressed cautious support if we had heard from the Lord. We were *trying* to hear.

We placed our home on the market despite the housing slump, completed the expensive medicals, and waited on the work visa. While waiting, a friend of both our sons, Joe, called to ask about using my utility trailer. He became quite alarmed when he heard that we were going to China and questioned whether it was plausible, especially since we would be away from our children and their families. It seemed like God was speaking directly to me. Wow! So unexpected! Shirley and I had prayed and pondered our China move but never wanted to be "... *weighed in the balances, and found wanting*" (Daniel 5:27, NKJV). Our heart was to do God's will. We had sold up, given up and moved continents many years before. If God was asking us to take this step, we would not shrink back. "... *'But my righteous one will live by faith. And I take no pleasure in the one who shrinks back.' But we do not belong to those who shrink back and are destroyed, but to those who have faith and are saved*" (Hebrews 10:38–39, NIV).

With our house on the market, we continued to wait. The China visas never materialized. Our "desire" to go to China began to wane over time. Shirley and I had an honest conversation and discovered that neither of us wanted to go to China, but we were willing to. We realized this was a test. "*He said, 'Do not lay your hand on the boy or do anything to him, for now I know that you fear God, seeing you have not withheld your son, your only son, from me'"* (Genesis 22:12, ESV). We released China prayerfully and a deep peace engulfed our hearts. A couple of years later, we hosted Chinese international high school students.

Still Unemployed but Debt-Free

We had been believing God that we could be debt-free with our home paid off despite being unemployed. It would take another miracle. One day Tom, our youngest son, called us. "Hey, Mom and Dad, I found a house just around the corner from you that you might like." Shirley and I looked at the home, which was undergoing renovations by the "flipper" (the person who had bought the house for a low price and was fixing it up to "flip" and make a profit). The "flipper" just happened to be a Christian man who headed up nearby Lakewood Retreat, a Christian campground where our sons attended and served over many years. We agreed on the price. We'd put our house on the market on August 21, 2013. A few months later, the impossible happened. A successful and respected realtor in our church, James Saffel, was the dual agent for the home we were selling and the one we hoped to buy. On December 13, 2013, we had two back-to-back closings, one selling our home and the other buying our new home. Miraculously, against the odds and sluggish housing market, we sold our home at top dollar and "bought down" for our new slightly *unfinished* home. Years of mortgage debt were eliminated in one day! We were still unemployed but now debt-free! God's miraculous provision! And we had a little extra cash to finish the "new" house renovations. *Thank You, Jesus! "Jesus looked at them and said, 'With man this is impossible, but not with God; all things are possible with God'"* (Mark 10:27, NIV).

Tim and his firefighter buddies laid laminate flooring, resurfaced kitchen countertops and did other fix-it projects. We moved into our new single-story home (which was just as spacious as our "old" double-story home). Instead of a pool, it had a wonderfully large L-shaped back porch. *Thank you, sons, for the part you played in helping us to move into our "new" home. You are indeed a blessing to us in so many ways, you and your amazing wives and kiddos. Thank you.*

The God of miracles had delivered us yet again and enabled us to *"mount up with wings as eagles"* and *soar above the storms* (Isaiah 40:31, KJV). All was calm, but I noticed a drop in the atmospheric pressure. Then heavy wind and rain were forecast....

Shirley's Reflections

During the seven-plus years it took Martin to complete his doctorate, we had very little downtime together. When he was teaching at Floyd Elementary School, I was substituting in the same school. I even took on a long-term assignment there. This enabled us to travel to and from school, which gave us some much-needed time together. We even had the same lunch break. School finished around 3:30 p.m. After school, we would stay to grade papers and plan for the next day. We left at 6:00 p.m. Martin had a set routine for studying. He rose very early in the mornings. Having a routine seemed to work well for us.

CHAPTER 15

Florida Later Days

(2014-2018)

Crisis Faced: Discipline – Good Teachers, Bad System
Crisis: Career – Job Bereavements
Storm: Tropical Cyclone – Rotating Storm

Humble Yourself
After completing scores of applications—a full-time job in itself—I realized that the school teaching position I was trying to avoid was a realistic and perhaps even a God-ordained option. Pride 101! *"Humble yourselves, therefore, under God's mighty hand, that he may lift you up in due time. Cast all your anxiety on him because he cares for you"* (1 Peter 5:6–7, NIV). *"Humble yourselves in the sight of the Lord, and He will lift you up"* (James 4:10, NKJV).

I was hired at Walden University in 2013 to work on doctoral committees and later at Liberty University in 2014 as an adjunct education professor to teach graduate students. I still needed a full-time position to help make ends meet plus cover medical. In early March 2014, I was hired as a sixth-grade teacher at a local middle school and then also given a seventh-grade science class. This meant I needed a middle school science endorsement quickly. Very quickly!

This change coincided with Shirley receiving an emergency call from her sister in England about her dad's dire health condition. She needed to fly to England immediately. (Sadly, her father died before she even boarded the plane.) To top it off, I had three days to study for the upcoming science exam. This was also our first year hosting Chinese students who attended a local Christian school. I now needed to fill Shirley's host role and provide meals, transportation and TLC. *Talk about the perfect stress storm!*

State Science Exam

My next-door neighbor, a sixth-grade science teacher, Cindy (not her real name), was a very capable science teacher and helped me settle in. *Thank you, Cindy.* An adjacent eighth-grade science teacher, Bill (not his real name), was also helpful and over an extended lunch at a local restaurant helped orient me to the exam requirements. He also loaned me some study materials and pointed me to online sources. *Thank you, Bill.* I had not delved into science at this level since high school about forty years ago in Africa.

The combination of stresses "leaked out" on our lone Chinese student, who was still adjusting to our home expectations. *Sorry, Hemingway. I should have handled this better.*

I drove down to Tampa, a large city in Florida's midwest coastal region. I was aware of the consequences of not passing the exam. I was prayed up and mentally overloaded but alert.

I received a printout as I left the exam center. PASS! I was ecstatic and praised God! The adrenaline rush was even greater than my lone parachute jump in New Zealand, and that was a thrill! God had enabled me to pass an exam for which I had not been formally trained. *Thank You, Jesus!* Miracles happen! Now the real learning would take place in the classroom as I studied the material and diligently prepared lessons. *"Study to shew thyself approved unto God, a workman that needeth not to be ashamed, rightly dividing the word of truth"* (2 Timothy 2:15, KJV).

New School Year (2015)

The first year ended and I had the summer to prepare for the following year. Teachers were assessed on their effectiveness, which depended on how well students performed on the end-of-quarter exams and teacher evaluation scores. I quickly learned which material was important and how best to teach it. I communicated the expectations clearly to students, provided direct instruction, and then guided hands-on activities that often required group collaborative work and HOTS (Higher Order Thinking Skills). I also planned lessons with Cindy, my neighbor science teacher. During my four and a quarter years teaching middle school, I was rated as a "highly" effective teacher and had some of the best science scores in the county along with my teacher compatriots. *Thank You, Jesus!*

Interrogation

I soon learned that action or inaction can have sudden and potentially severe consequences. I communicated high expectations in behavior and academics to all my students. However, one student challenged the expectations and was required to call home. The call was supposed to be brief but became overextended and disturbed the class. I subsequently intervened and *terminated* the call. The student was escorted to the office by the school's resource officer. It was the day before the four-day Thanksgiving break.

I made a call home to his mother between classes and explained exactly what I had done to end the phone conversation. She began pouring out her troubles about her son, saying how rebellious and out of control he was at home. However, a little later, I was called to the principal's office and remained in "isolation" for the remainder of the day as the student had called home with fabrications. Both the student and parent complained.

I had to push back hard on the looming cloud of heaviness and the "what if?" questions. Was I about to lose my job? Would I end up in prison? I decided to simply trust the Lord in this trial (as in every trial). Monday rolled in like an unwelcome steamroller. I was later informed by the principal that he had finished his investigation and found no credible evidence to support the accusations. I was cleared of all wrongdoing. *Thank You, Jesus. "Fear not, for I am with you; be not dismayed, for I am your God. I will strengthen you, yes, I will help you, I will uphold you with My righteous right hand"* (Isaiah 41:10, NKJV).

Broken and Restored

One day a seventh-grade girl was acting out in class. She was deeply upset about something and did not respond to normal appeals to stay on task. Instead, she dramatically burst out with, "My father's broken his back!" I was alarmed and moved with compassion. Why was this student carrying such a heavy burden? Was her father's back broken? I decided to call home and explain what was happening in the classroom with this non-compliant student.

The girl's mother answered the phone. I quickly discovered that this mother was a strong believer and that her husband had been on workman's compensation because of his back for many years. He was bedridden and in excruciating pain, unable to move. The relationship between the father and daughter had deteriorated over time largely because of the father's pain and frustration over his daughter's non-compliance at home. I recognized my limits as a believer in public education, but I did share that she and I had a common faith and that I would be happy to assist in any way possible outside of school. I told her that my wife and I prayed healing prayers for people.

The mother called back about a week later and informed me that her husband was in the hospital. She asked if I would come and pray for him. I arrived at the local hospital and introduced myself. The daughter was there and seemed surprised to see me. I prayed a healing prayer and left. There did not seem to be any immediate change in the father's condition. However, there was a positive change in the daughter's attitude and behavior at school. I think she saw my care and concern for her father.

I received another call about two weeks later. Would I come to their home and pray for the father again? Shirley accompanied me this time. The man was bedridden and had to crawl on his hands and knees if he wanted to use the bathroom. The only means of transportation he had was by ambulance. The hospital treatment had not worked. He was still in excruciating pain and despair. We encouraged him with healing scriptures and prayed for him. Again there was no immediate healing manifestation. The father was eager to receive prayer the following week. I agreed but gave him homework. I sensed that healing was not being manifested because of some "spiritual" blockage. I told the father to ask the Holy Spirit to show him any broken relationships in his life and then begin the restoration process by reaching out to the individuals.

I received a call from the student's mother partway through the week. She was ecstatic. Although her husband was still bedbound, his whole countenance had changed. He was doing his homework and had reached out to his adult children. I had not known that he had adult children or that his relationship with them was in tatters. The broken relationships were being mended.

Shirley and I arrived late to their home on Saturday afternoon. The girl's father was in surprisingly good spirits. Shirley and I asked if we could anoint their home with oil and pray over it. They readily agreed. The girl's mother led us from room to room. We anointed each room with oil and prayed prayers of deliverance as we waited on the Holy Spirit's leading. We then went back to the father's room, anointed him with oil, and prayed prayers of deliverance and healing over him. Still nothing. We knew God was and is the Healer and followed the wife through the front door to our vehicle in front of their double-wide garage.

We were saying goodbye when suddenly the double-wide garage door started creaking open. We peered into the darkness of the garage. Out shuffled the wife's husband. The bedbound man with excruciating back pain who had been unable to walk was upright and walking. Pain free! He was in his striped pajamas.

"As soon as you laid hands on me today, I felt warmth go through my body. I felt bones shifting in my back. I knew the Holy Spirit was healing me," the father exclaimed joyously.

A few months later this man packed a moving trailer himself and moved his wife and daughter up north to be with his grown children. *Thank You, Jesus, for healing this man completely and for restoring relationships. Amen.* "*Having therefore these promises, dearly beloved,* **let us cleanse ourselves from all filthiness of the flesh and spirit,** *perfecting holiness in the fear of God*" (2 Corinthians 7:1, KJV, emphasis added).

DNA Truth

I enjoyed my time teaching at the middle school. However, one demanding full-time teaching position plus two demanding part-time university positions left little family time. I had to manage my time carefully and still leave a little "gas in the tank" for Shirley and home life.

I was a hands-on teacher and introduced fertilized chick eggs in an incubator. The students were excited about science and engaged in learning. The students monitored the incubator temperature and learned about chick development. They knew that the chick's life began at conception in its embryonic stage. I asked students what would happen if the incubator was not set at the correct temperature or if an egg was dropped on the floor. The students were aghast. They clearly understood the chick's life would end and that it would be a travesty. They also understood that deliberately killing a chick was to abort the chick. I was using chicks to show how precious life is. All life. Including human life.

I connected the chick eggs with science topics in the classroom. DNA was the topic of one such science lesson. I explained that DNA (deoxyribonucleic acid) was the molecule in a cell that carried genetic information. However, a student objected to the scientific facts when I stated that DNA does not change. Soon a "squad" of girls echoed her opinion. Vociferously!

I had carefully presented the lesson knowing that students were being bombarded with LGBTQ and gender fluidity messages, mainly through their social media.

I thought a jingle would help students learn. Wrong! The lyrics of the first verse went like this: "A rooster is a rooster, not a hen; a rooster is a rooster, not a hen; a rooster with a booster's still a rooster; a rooster is a rooster, not a hen."

The next day I had an unexpected classroom assessment visit from the assistant principal. My heart was pounding. She sat at the right back of the classroom, tablet in hand. This was serious. My first thought was that the disenchanted "squad" had exercised their student rights and complained about my DNA teaching. I thought my "goose was cooked." However, I was not going to change my lesson.

I had a flashback to my early years teaching at Shabani Primary School in Shabani (now Zvishavane), Zimbabwe. I had posted an appeal on the teachers' lunchroom bulletin board titled, "Please Let Us Play Marbles." The school headmaster (principal) and teachers did not allow students to "be kids" at recess since they feared they would be hurt. They could not even play marbles, a popular activity among kids. I acted as a reporter and reported their feelings to the teachers. One teacher was so incensed that she "tore" my letter from the teachers' bulletin board and marched with it in hand to the headmaster's office. I was immediately called to his office and read the "riot act." Ironically, a few months later, the school board *allowed* children to be children.

Back to reality—what would happen after this teacher evaluation? Was my position on the chopping block?

As I wrapped up the DNA portion of the lesson, the "squad" sprang into action. They voiced the exact questions they had angrily voiced the previous day. The "trap" was sprung. However, I explained the basic components of DNA and related it to chicks. A chick was a chick. A hen was a hen. A rooster was a rooster. You could not change the DNA of cells to make a hen a rooster or a rooster a hen.

Toward the end of the lesson, the assistant principal stood and started speaking. She spoke directly to the "squad." "Dr. Ratcliffe is correct. These are scientific facts that cannot be altered. A human may add or remove appendages, but that does not alter their DNA." *Thank You, Jesus!* "*So God created man in his own image, in the image of God he created him; male and female he created them*" (Genesis 1:27, ESV).

I was relieved and grateful for the assistant principal's standing by me. This was the same assistant principal who transitioned behaviorally "difficult" students to my class. I asked her why she did this. She explained, "There is peace in your classroom. Students learn and behave better when they feel safe and at peace." I was thankful for her support. It was not an easy ride teaching middle schoolers, but they could tell I loved them even though I was firm on expectations and challenged them to set high but reasonable personal and academic goals. The elongated poster slogan on the left side wall was, "Attitude is a Little Thing that Makes a BIG difference." How appropriate for every grade level (and every phase of life). "*Peace I leave with you; my peace I give to you. Not as the world gives do I give to you. Let not your hearts be troubled, neither let them be afraid*" (John 14:27, ESV). "*Sanctify them by the truth; your word is truth*" (John 17:17, NIV).

Honorary Black Belt

Mr. B (not his real name) was a highly accomplished martial arts instructor and the taekwondo teacher at the middle school where I taught science. I conferred with him about a science lesson demonstrating Newton's second law of motion. (Newton's second law of motion states that the force (F) acting on an object is equal to the mass (m) of an object times its acceleration (a). This law is often expressed as F=ma.) Mr. B helped me refresh my wood-breaking techniques. I practiced breaking several sections of wood under his watchful eye. I soon brushed up on the technique and demonstrated it for every lesson outside under cover near the lunchroom. My students as well as those from two other sixth-grade science classes were in attendance. Students gasped audibly when this unlikely older gentleman smashed through a solid piece of wood. Overall, about 300 students witnessed the wood breaking and Newton's second law in action. I used the occasion to teach the principles of persistence and focus, encouraging students to "look beyond their immediate problems to possible solutions" and not to give up on their dreams. Mr. B was so impressed with the demonstrations and lessons that he awarded me an honorary black belt. *Thank you, Mr. B; I had a lifelong dream to have a black belt.* "*Delight yourself in the Lord, and he will give you the desires of your heart*" (Psalm 37:4, ESV). I did not report back that the "boxer's" bone at the bottom of my right-hand pinkie may have been compromised. Ouch!

Teacher Healed

One retirement-age lady teacher, very evidently a Christian, told me she hoped to go overseas on a mission trip in the summer. However, one knee was extremely painful, and it seemed that she would not be able to go. I asked if I could pray for her knee. She agreed. I asked her to place her hand on her knee where it was hurting and if I could place my hand on her hand. She willingly agreed. We agreed in prayer for the complete healing of her knee. I then asked her to do something she had not been previously able to do. She walked to the front left of the classroom, and then to the front right. Her beaming smile told it all. Jesus had healed her. Completely. Instantly. Pain-free. Able to walk unhindered. She later enjoyed a wonderful overseas missions trip and climbed many high mountains completely pain-free. *Thank You, Jesus.* "*Again I say to you that if two of you agree on earth concerning anything that they ask, it will be done for them by My Father in heaven*" (Matthew 18:19, NKJV). "*But he was pierced for our transgressions, he was crushed for our iniquities; the punishment that brought us peace was on him, and by his wounds we are healed*" (Isaiah 53:5, NIV).

Overload

The long school days, evenings, early mornings and working weekends were taking their toll. My heart rate slowed to thirty-five beats per minute or even slower. I felt devoid of energy at times. Three jobs with a combined eighty-five-hour-plus work week were just too much. The problem was that teaching provided security—a steady income and good medical coverage. Shirley and I began praying about dropping my full-time position and doing two part-time adjunct positions, one at Walden University and the other with Liberty University. However, these part-time positions offered zero security or benefits.

Shirley and I were in the valley of decision. The updraft of God's grace kept us buoyant *above the storms*, but it was time for a change. Peals of thunder crashed overhead, and brilliant light flashes lit up the evening skies....

Shirley's Reflections

I did not do much substituting when we hosted Chinese international students. We had seven over the years. I did sometimes substitute at the school across the road where our students went. The times coincided with their school, so I was conveniently able to get them to and from school and to their afternoon activities. I did on occasion substitute for Martin's class when he needed an extra study day or if he had exams. God always made a way for us.

CHAPTER 16

Florida Latest Days

(2018-Today)

Crisis Faced: Walking on Water – Taking God at His Word
Crisis: Retirement – God IS Our Source
Storm: Thunderstorms – Lightning, Thunder, Heavy Rain

Stepping out of the Boat
I had still not "stepped out of the boat" at the end of the 2018 school year. I tried every which way to make things work in my mind but could not find a resolution. Shirley said, "Just quit. God will take care of us as He always has." However, I knew quitting meant "walking on water" by faith where there were no visible signs of support. At almost sixty-two years of age, I still had almost five years to go before Social Security and Medicare kicked in. A lot was riding on this decision, especially the medical coverage for my wife and me.

I sought prayerful counsel from our "new" pastor who gave me a word, Exodus 14:13–14: "*And Moses said to the people, 'Do not be afraid. Stand still, and see the salvation of the Lord, which He will accomplish for you today. For the Egyptians whom you see today, you shall see again no more forever. The Lord will fight for you, and you shall hold your peace'*" (NKJV).

This word resonated deeply with me and boosted my faith as it was the same word God had given me when my position at Southeastern

University had been cut several years prior. I prayed, sought the Lord and fasted. Nothing. There was no substitute for *getting out* of the boat and *walking* by faith. "*And Peter answered Him and said, 'Lord, if it is You, command me to come to You on the water.' So He said, 'Come.' And when Peter had come down out of the boat, he walked on the water to go to Jesus. But when he saw that the wind was boisterous, he was afraid; and beginning to sink he cried out, saying, 'Lord, save me!' And immediately Jesus stretched out His hand and caught him...*" (Matthew 14:28–31, NKJV). "*But do you want to know, O foolish man, that faith without works is dead?*" (James 2:20, NKJV).

Then I did what I often do when facing difficult situations. I sat down, listened to the Holy Spirit, then wrote a song that many people request at Hillbilly music and sing-along meetings.1 I titled the song, "Keep Walking on the Water." Lyrics to the chorus follow:

I'm walking on the water
Not sitting in the boat
I'm walking on the water
I'm still afloat
My God is with me
Beckons me to come
I'm walking on the water
My time's not done

Online Adjunct Professor

The decision to depart from middle school teaching with its pay and health insurance "securities" was agonizing. Finally, one summer morning when Shirley and I were driving near the middle school, we decided to "take the plunge." God had given us His word. We'd sought counsel. I had made the principal aware of the possibility of not returning. He understood. However, we could not keep the school waiting any longer for a definitive decision. We stopped at the school, and I asked to see the principal.

The principal thanked me for my service with deep and genuine thanks and gave me the key to pick up my personal effects still in the

---

1 Leonard O'Donnell, the leader of a local "Hillbilly" band, explains that the "Hillbilly" style of music was common to the Appalachian people and that "Hillbilly" refers to the style of music.

classroom. The word spread like wildfire even though most teachers were not on campus. Staff and teachers came to my classroom, some teary-eyed. We talked and hugged. It was a wonderful feeling to feel appreciated, yet I was also saddened to say goodbye. I sensed the presence of the Holy Spirit and peace. Somehow, God would provide the income and medical coverage we needed in the transition years to Social Security and beyond. *"Even to your old age and gray hairs I am he, I am he who will sustain you. I have made you and I will carry you; I will sustain you and I will rescue you"* (Isaiah 46:4, NIV).

My recent "promotion" to "Subject Matter Expert" (SME) for the on-line School Administration course at Liberty University was a factor in the decision. This was another "step of faith" since fellow peers had warned that there was too much responsibility with the position. I politely declined the SME position and then received a call from the individual doing the hiring. "We believe you are well matched to this position and will do an excellent job. We have handpicked you for the position." I decided to push all doubt (and peer counsel) aside and take a step of faith. That was several years ago. At the time of writing this book, I am still the SME for this course and have received strong positive evaluations from supervisors and students alike. *All praise goes to Jesus! "But you, O Lord, are a shield about me, my glory, and the lifter of my head"* (Psalm 3:3, ESV).

China Mission

The associate pastor of our church asked if I was interested in going to China with him and his youngest son. I prayed and felt God's peace, then prepared for our departure in late September 2019—just before the outbreak of the devastating COVID-19 pandemic.

God had given me a dream about our destination, Chengdu, months before. In the dream, I was in a vehicle going up a gradual incline. At the top of the rise was a massive city blanketed with an ominous heavy black cloud. I realized that God was showing me the spiritual condition of Chengdu, which prompted my forty-day partial fast. I knew I could not depend on my strength, only His. I prepared personal materials during this time suitable for our Chinese brothers and sisters.

Driving from Chengdu International Airport to our hotel room was like reliving my dream. A black ominous cloud hung over the city.

We arrived the week of the seventieth anniversary of communism in China. A massive military parade had been planned in Beijing as well as in other cities. Everyone was "on edge," including the "underground" churches we were slated to visit. All but one "church" canceled on us. However, God showed up gloriously in the high-rise apartment "underground" home church. These people understood the cost of discipleship and the possibility of losing their job, pension and house, plus facing criminal charges and jail time for violating the demands of the communist government. One area pastor had recently been imprisoned for nine years for "inciting to subvert state power" and "illegal business operations."

About thirty-five people were packed into the tiny apartment. The service began at 9:00 a.m., broke for lunch, and continued late into the afternoon. The local "pastor/leader" led the service using modern technology and an overhead screen. The spiritual energy in the room during praise and worship was palpable. The associate pastor from my church spoke a few hours later with the aid of an interpreter, an English-speaking Chinese college student who attended university in Germany. She was not a Christian but was sympathetic to the cause. He brought a timely message.

Lunch consisted of several bowls with various vegetables and meats. The challenging part for me was communal dining. Overall, the meal was enjoyed by all. After lunch, we enjoyed more worship, then the leader asked our team to pray for members. I stood at the front of the room. People came up for prayer while the college student interpreter interpreted. In total, about eight to ten people came to me for prayer. Some had multiple ailments. Requests for prayer covered the spectrum from various serious ailments to back and neck pains. The Holy Spirit was tangibly present. God did amazing healing miracles through me that day. Everyone who came for prayer was healed. All glory goes to Jesus, the Author and Finisher of my faith. *Thank You, Jesus, for Your manifest presence. "…And the power of the Lord was with Jesus to heal the sick"* (Luke 5:17, NIV).

Later, on my departure from China, the American China mission host who had invited us felt God had a "word" for me about a full-time healing ministry. I have received many such "words" over the years and am always ready to pray for anyone who needs prayer. I also carry anointing oil with me. *"Bless the Lord, O my soul; and all that is within me, bless His holy name! Bless the Lord, O my soul, and forget not all His benefits: who forgives all your iniquities, who heals all your diseases"* (Psalm 103:1–3, NKJV).

Healing Desire and Anointing

Shirley and I desire to pray healing prayers for anyone in need. This desire began early in our walk with Christ in Zimbabwe and was fueled by testimonies of God healing people we knew. Later we received healing training through Charles and Frances Hunter, Dr. Randy Clark, Dr. Henry Wright (Excellent Way), Drs. Paul and Claire Hollis (deliverance), and others, plus from numerous books on healing. We also became "ordained" under Joan Hunter Ministries.

Shirley and I host a monthly meeting at home. We call the meeting "Healing Flames," symbolized by the flame lily, *Gloriosa superba*, the national flower of Zimbabwe. We believe with Dr. Michelle Strydom and others that "No Disease Is Incurable" (the title of her book and DVD series). God is the Healer regardless of the need, whether physical, emotional, spiritual or any other kind. *"…For I am the Lord, who heals you"* (Exodus 15:26, NIV). *"But to you who fear My name the Sun of Righteousness shall arise with healing in His wings; and you shall go out and grow fat like stall-fed calves"* (Malachai 4:2, NKJV).

Professor Touched by Healing Prayer

One of my Liberty University supervisors was a lady who owned horses. One day she received a serious injury when a horse kicked her in the face. I called to see how she was doing but was directed to voicemail. I left a healing prayer message. "Father, I pray for Dr. Y. I speak to her condition, in Jesus' name, and command broken bones to be healed and all pain to leave her body. I speak to concussion and brain trauma—peace, be still. I release Your healing anointing, in Jesus' name." Dr. Y later communicated that she was deeply moved by the prayer and played it over and over. God began to miraculously accelerate the healing process. *Thank You, Jesus. "If you ask anything in My name, I will do it"* (John 14:14, NKJV).

Online Student Healed

Jesus healed a centurion's servant without being physically present to lay a hand on him. Jesus has empowered us to do the same. *"Then Jesus said to the centurion, 'Go your way; and as you have believed, so let it be done for you.' And his servant was healed that same hour"* (Matthew 8:13, NKJV). *"He sent His word and healed them, and delivered them from their destructions"* (Psalm 107:20, NKJV).

One graduate student had difficulty turning in work on time. I called him to see if I could be of help. He explained that he had been a paratrooper in the military and his back was messed up from too many jumps. The excruciating pain prevented him from sitting to do his assignments. He had severe pain on both sides of his back caused by slipped discs. The Holy Spirit completely healed this student over the phone. He was able to bend beyond where he could bend before. He could climb stairs pain-free, which he could not do before. And he could sit down, pain-free, which he could not do before. *Thank You, Jesus!* The student turned in his completed assignment shortly thereafter.

Heifer Kick

Tom, our youngest son, loves cows and grazes them on friendly neighbors' farms. In August 2020, a steer he was attempting to corral suddenly kicked him, forcefully ripping his pectoral muscle clean off the humerus and causing excruciating pain. This rendered his arm useless. Thankfully a surgeon was able to reattach the muscle to the bone with titanium screws. God answered our prayers. *Thank You, Jesus!*

Close to Home

Healing and deliverance are not just for others. Sometimes *we* need healing prayer. For the first few months of 2020, Shirley experienced anxiety and needed prayer. We found this to be a process and learned that frequent and intensive prayers for healing and deliverance eventually yielded results. Shirley later shared her testimony with a group going through a course entitled "Breaking Free" at our church. Her testimony was an encouragement to many. *"For God has not given us a spirit of fear, but of power and of love and of a sound mind"* (2 Timothy 1:7, NKJV).

Cardiac Arrest

In October 2021, Tim, our oldest son, developed two massive embolisms, a complication of recent surgery. The doctor told Tim's wife that people in his condition do not leave the hospital. The outlook was grim.

We immediately began praying and shared the request with intercessors globally. That was on a Sunday evening. He was rushed to a catheterization (cath) lab to begin meds to try to dissolve the clots. Tim's life was in the balance. The following day there was not much change. On Tuesday, however, things were looking up. The technician who took before and after pictures of Tim's heart burst into the hospital room and exclaimed excitedly, "This looks like a new heart. This is not the same heart I saw on Sunday. I can't believe what I'm looking at." She burst into tears. Tim's heart was completely healed, including one leaky heart valve, all through the power of prayer. *Thank You, Jesus!* "*The effective, fervent prayer of a righteous man avails much*" (James 5:16b, NKJV).

Africa Trip

Liam, my youngest brother, decided on his sixtieth birthday present. He wanted to return to his roots in Africa, specifically Cape Town, South Africa, where he'd gone to medical school, and then his main high school, Fort Victoria High School, now called Masvingo High School, in Zimbabwe. He invited his surviving siblings and their spouses to accompany him. And he generously offered to fund the entire trip, first class all the way! *That's my brother!*

Shirley and I were immediately ecstatic and dread-filled simultaneously. Ecstatic because we would be together celebrating Liam's sixtieth birthday as he desired, and in conflict because we had very strong convictions about *not* taking the COVID-19 vaccines. Then I whispered a prayer. "Jesus, please show me what to do." I had hardly whispered the prayer and was walking to my office when the Lord "dropped" a Scripture reference in my spirit: "Matthew 3:15."

I knew what Matthew 3:15 said since the Lord had spoken to me through this verse years prior as a young man when I was considering baptism by immersion. "*Jesus replied, 'Let it be so now; it is proper for us to do this to fulfill all righteousness.' Then John consented*" (Matthew 3:15, NIV). I immediately felt released in my spirit to accept my brother's invitation, even if it meant receiving the COVID vaccine shots. After all, my love for my brother was and is stronger than my very strong feelings against these "vaccines." Shirley decided later to follow suit and have the necessary jabs for the trip.

In twenty-eight days, we made nine air trips, one amazing train trip on Rovos Rail, the "world's most luxurious train in Africa," and multiple road trips. We decided to leave a little earlier than Liam and return a little later. Since this was such a rare gift, and we hardly ever returned to Africa, we decided to invite Shirley's younger sister in England to join her older sister in South Africa for a six-day "sisters'" reunion. Shirley and her sisters Jane and Lee had a wonderfully rich and quality time catching up on many years apart.

I spent an evening with my best man, Peter, and his wife. We invited the Holy Spirit's presence and had a glorious evening of prayer and fellowship.

Shirley and I then flew to the Victoria Falls for a tour, a desire of Shirley's, and compliments of my brother. *Thank you so much, Liam. You have been and are such a blessing in our lives!* We enjoyed an amazing two days exploring the world's largest falls.

Payback

Before leaving for Africa, I contacted my education book publisher and asked if they would like to donate copies to schools and universities in Africa. They very generously donated two boxes of my book, *Schools That Make the Grade: What Effective Schools Do to Improve Student Achievement.* The only problem was the prohibitive duty costs. We did not have the ten to fifteen thousand dollars for import fees, but rather than put this cost on to the recipients, we decided to absorb the risk and personally transport the books. *This was a significant step of faith....*

We landed in Johannesburg, South Africa, with our regular baggage and two additional heavy suitcases filled with books. We were standing in the passport line when the booth in front had a sudden "technical" issue, and we were moved to the next controller. I had sensed a deep heaviness in my spirit before being redirected. The lady at the first booth looked oppressed and unfriendly. The next controller was friendly and processed us quickly. *Thank You, Jesus!*

A few minutes later we approached the immigration section. Astonishingly, no one was manning the station, and we walked right through to the airport exit—with the books. *Thank You, Jesus.* Several days later when we arrived at the Victoria Falls International Airport, they gave us the "red carpet" treatment and waved us through. *Thank You, Jesus!* God honored our faith and made a way for us through immigration in South Africa and Zimbabwe. "*No temptation has overtaken you except such as is common to man; but God is faithful, who will not allow you to be tempted beyond what you are able, but with the temptation will also make the way of escape, that you may be able to bear it*" (1 Corinthians 10:13, NKJV). A member of the Zimbabwean parliament had obtained a letter for me explaining that the books were for the Zimbabwean government. The letter arrived after we had landed in South Africa and before our flight to Zimbabwe. As it turned out, we did not need the letter. *Thank You, Jesus!*

The Zimbabwe member of Parliament whom I had been working through arranged for a local member of Parliament to meet me at the hotel and pick up the books. Amazingly, he met us at our hotel just as we arrived from the Victoria Falls International Airport, and he immediately left on the several hundred-mile journey to the Zimbabwe capital, Harare, where he gave the books to our contact person. We were thrilled. I felt a deep honor in "paying back" to Zimbabwe with my best fruits for all Zimbabwe (and formerly Rhodesia) had done for me. My prayer was and is that these books would transform schools and universities throughout Zimbabwe (and Africa) for the glory of God.

I was also able to "sow" books with a college friend who had risen to prominence in the South African government. Later I "sowed" books at Somabhula Primary School and Masvingo High School, schools I had attended as a youth. I also "sowed" a book at Umniati (Munyati) Primary where I had been the headmaster (principal). Several other books were sown to universities and to individuals we met on our journey.

Our trip culminated in our hometown, Fort Victoria (now Masvingo), with a school reunion. We enjoyed amazing Zimbabwe stone accommodations with thatched roofs near the Great Zimbabwe tourist attraction that we knew so well. We caught up with friends, and I even sang a song I'd written one afternoon titled *"Nitor Donec Supero,"* our school motto ("I strive until I overcome"), summarizing our family's collective journey, to the Johnny Cash tune of "I Walk the Line."

Pickleball

I enjoy pickleball and am a certified coach able to teach beginners to advanced students. I now have a nice display of medals, mainly from local events. I have developed a Pickleball Placement Matrix visual titled "Pickleball at the Cross" that I use when coaching others. I explore avenues to integrate biblical concepts into pickleball that will point students to the "cross" in pickleball that is down the middle of the court toward the baseline, and more importantly, to the cross of Christ. *"Then he called the crowd to him along with his disciples and said: 'Whoever wants to be my disciple must deny themselves and take up their **cross** and follow me'"* (Mark 8:34, NIV, emphasis added). *"For the message of the **cross** is foolishness to those who are perishing, but to us who are being saved it is the power of God"* (1 Corinthians 1:18, NIV, emphasis added).

Precious Gifts

Our two sons love Jesus, their wives, their kiddos and their country. And they love their parents. They and their wives have blessed us with precious grandchildren. They have also been generous with costly gifts. One very special gift from Tom and Tim in 2009 was a thirteen-foot boat in mint condition. Years later I loaned my utility trailer to Tim after the hurricanes, as he had so much cleanup to do. My trailer was a workhorse but rusty and bent with dried-out and cracked floorboards. It was long overdue for some TLC. For Christmas 2024, Tim completely transformed my old, rusty and broken-down trailer into a brand-new-looking trailer. His son Kai and Tom's son Carver helped. And they kept the "good" secret until the gift was unveiled on Christmas Day. *Thank you, Tim (and Kai and Carver), and thank you, Tom, for helping to fund the project.* What tremendous love from my sons and grandsons. *I am deeply grateful to God for my loving wife, sons, daughters-in-law and all the grandkiddos. You are an amazing gift from God and enrich my life deeply.*

Two Quick Boating Stories

After praying and discussing the matter with my sons, I returned the boat as a gift on Father's Day, 2025, as per our discussions. I wrote an accompanying letter of appreciation detailing what had been done to the boat and what still needed to be done. It said in part: "Sixteen years ago today, on Father's Day, 2009, you blessed me with a boat. It was one of the best days of my life. This boat and the refurbished utility trailer are/ were among my most prized gifts." I ended the letter with the following:

Mom and I have had some wonderful, hilarious and even pre-carious memories on the boat over the years. We've enjoyed launching at Bayport and exploring the surrounding waters.

Boat Story 1: On a balmy, hot day, we decided to take a dip not too far from our launch site. We were both able to get out of the boat. The water was clear and refreshing and chest-deep. No sharks. When we tried to gain reentry (one at a time), the side of the boat dipped almost to the water level, then popped up when we let go. It was virtually impossible to get into the boat. We decided to use the large cooler in the boat as a footstool. Mom went first. I tried to stabilize the boat from the other side. Mom made several unsuccessful attempts. The cooler remained submerged as long as both feet were securely on it. However, as soon as one leg lifted, trying to climb into the boat, the cooler popped to the surface, resulting in an unsuccessful boarding attempt and being dunked in the water. Still no sharks! Eventually, Mom made it and rolled over the side of the boat. Now it was my turn. The problem was that Mom was in the boat, so there was no one to stabilize it. The boat dipped and rocked back and forth, and the cooler popped up several times until I finally slithered over the side, quite exhausted. At least we made it back in the boat—and rescued the floating cooler!

Boat Story 2: On another occasion, we were launching the boat at Bayport. The place was crowded, so we had to keep our place in line and pretend that we knew what we were doing. No-body likes to be held up, especially on a hot day. I readied the boat for launching, removed the secure strap (which I hadn't on another occasion—oops!), and backed down into the water. I was so proud of myself. The launch went well. I backed up straight, released the boat, which Mom secured with a rope to the dock, and pulled the boat trailer out of the water. Then I noticed the strangest thing. The back of the boat seemed to be lower than usual in the water. Strange! I clambered out of the SUV to investigate. The next launcher was becoming impatient. Then I saw the problem. The boat was sinking. Oh no! It was about one-third filled with water at the back. I quickly backed the trailer under the boat and pulled it up out of the water. The SUV and trailer were still on the inclined launch pad. (I did not want to lose my spot in line.) The culprit, a missing plug at the back of the boat, had welcomed the brackish water into my boat. Sink! Sink! Gravity eventually forced the water out of the hole in the rear of the boat. I secured the missing plug, checked it multiple times, re-launched the boat, then moved it out of the way so that other boat launchers could enjoy what was left of the day. Somehow, we managed to still enjoy our day. However, we never strayed far from terra firma—just in case!

Of course, not all our ventures were as eventful. Most trips were pleasant. I even earned my safety boater's license. However, it's now your turn to make memories. Hopefully, they will be of a non-eventful variety, as you are both more skilled at boating than I. God will show you what to do with the boat when it's time to release it. No strings attached, just like when you both blessed me with the boat.☺

Lots of love and great boating memories,
Dad

"When he had finished speaking, he said to Simon, 'Put out into deep water, and let down the nets for a catch'" (Luke 5:4, NIV).

Ever-Loving

My wife has been an unwavering support by my side since our marriage on April 25, 1981. She always ends her cards and letters with "Your ever-loving wife, Shirley." *Shirley, you have been a blessing to me, a gift from* the Lord. "*She is more precious than rubies, and all the things you may desire cannot compare with her*" (Proverbs 3:15, NKJV). It would take another volume to begin to tell of all her many wonderful attributes.

Reflection

God has been and continues to be so good to us. God is faithful. When "man" messes up, God can salvage the mess and make something beautiful. That is my story. Our story. The original vision of coming to America to serve alongside my friend and pastor in full-time ministry shattered, but God has restored and led us for over forty years in the land that we now love and call home—*America the beautiful!*

It took obedience, sacrifice and faith to leave our family and beloved Zimbabwe and travel to the unknown in America. The road has been difficult at times with challenges on every front, but God has faithfully led us through the years and through many perilous times. We have felt abandoned, unable to "fit in" at times, lonely and even fearful, but we have never abandoned our faith in God or been abandoned by Him. We have clung to His precious promises and continue to believe God has a plan for our lives and posterity. We have taught our sons, grandchildren and others that God is faithful. "*But the Lord is faithful, and he will strengthen you and protect you from the evil one*" (2 Thessalonians 3:3, NIV). "*So do not fear, for I am with you; do not be dismayed, for I am your God. I will strengthen you and help you; I will uphold you with my righteous right hand*" (Isaiah 41:10, NIV). Indeed, God has graciously provided for us through the frequent times of uncertainty as we have pilgrimaged through a "foreign" land. "*I have been young, and now am old; yet I have not seen the righteous forsaken, nor his descendants begging bread*" (Psalm 37:25, NKJV).

Our sons are established in the land and have virtuous, godly wives, amazing "kiddos" and good jobs. They, too, have their struggles but can build on our faith and legacy and continue to do great exploits for God. We hand the baton of faith to our sons, Timothy James and Thomas Luke. We have not been "perfect" parents by any means, but we have done our best to raise them lovingly in light of God's Word and especially Ephesians 6:4: "*And you, fathers, do not provoke your children to wrath, but bring them up in the training and admonition of the Lord*" (NJKV).

Our prayer for our sons and for *all* who read this book is that you will *trust God no matter what* and that you will *soar above the storms.* We urge you to meet with Jesus daily in your devotional time and often during the day. Listen to His voice, those inner promptings. Seek confirmation from His Word. Obey the Lord. As the refrain from the old hymn "Trust and Obey" goes:

> Trust and obey
> For there's no other way
> To be happy in Jesus,
> But to trust and obey

Yes, God has been faithful and true. He called me from Africa over forty years ago to serve Him in America. I have stood in faith on the Bible verse He quickened to me: "*From the east I summon a bird of prey; from a far-off land, a man to fulfill my purpose. What I have said, that I will bring about; what I have planned, that I will do*" (Isaiah 46:11, NIV). My faithful and ever-loving wife, Shirley, has been by my side. Together, as we step into the wonderful future God has for us in our latter days, I am reminded of the phrase I completed as part of a sermon challenge. "Forever is a *gloriously* long time." *Come, Lord Jesus!* The best is yet to come!

Closing Words

God's ways are not our ways. God has taught us to rely on Him and His Word. We have learned lessons in the "fire" that we might not have learned otherwise. We have experienced, and continue to experience, God's protection, guidance, deliverance, healing, miracles and more. We are so thankful for His grace and mercy throughout our lives. Like the eagle, He has enabled us to fly *above the storms. Thank You, Jesus!*

What about you, dear reader? God loves you and wants you to spend eternity with Him. Do you love Him with *all* your heart? Do you *know* that you have eternal life? Are you living by *faith*? Are you flying *above the storms*? "*I write these things to you who believe in the name of the Son of God so that you may **know** that you have eternal life*"

(1 John 5:13, NIV, emphasis added). *"For it is by grace you have been saved, through faith—and this is not from yourselves, it is the gift of God"* (Ephesians 2:8, NIV, emphasis added).

You can settle the matter by talking to God. Do it now…. Here is a suggested prayer to help you get started: "Father, I am a sinner. Please forgive me for all my sins. I receive the gift of eternal life through Your Son, Jesus Christ. Jesus, please come into my heart. Wash all my sins away with Your precious blood. Help me to live for You. Fill me with Your Holy Spirit and help me to *soar above the storms.* In Jesus' name, I pray. Amen."

God bless you, dear friend. If you prayed this prayer (or something similar) earnestly from your heart, you are saved and on your way to heaven! Give Jesus first place in your life. Live daily for Him. Quickly confess your sins. Share the good news of the gospel, including your personal testimony, with others—just as I have shared my testimony with you in this book. Find a Bible-believing church and start growing in God's Word.

I wrote the following lyrics inspired by Isaiah 40:31 and have sung the upbeat repetitious jingle to young and old alike over many years: "Fly like an eagle, not like a seagull, not like a turkey or a crow." *"But they that wait upon the Lord shall renew their strength; they shall mount up with wings as eagles; they shall run, and not be weary; and they shall walk, and not faint"* (Isaiah 40:31, KJV).

Now it's your turn to "fly like an eagle and *soar above the storms"*!

Shirley's Reflections

We could never have imagined the wild journey the Lord took us on. We were and are on fire for Jesus and always want to do His will. We have had highs and lows, but this one thing I know is that Jesus will never leave or forsake us. We have followed Him to the best of our ability and given Him our "yes." *"Trust in the Lord with all your heart, and do not lean on your own understanding. In all your ways acknowledge him, and he will make straight your paths"* (Proverbs 3:5–6, ESV). *"The heart of man plans his way, but the Lord establishes his steps"* (Proverbs 16:9, ESV). Our God is able and faithful.

Epilogue

As Shirley and I grow older together, we realize more and more how blessed we are. God has given us a country that has adopted us, a home, two amazing sons and their wives, five healthy grandchildren, a church, a healing ministry (in our home), friends, "work" for our hands, health and days ahead to work for the Lord. Every day is a gift from God. Revelation 2:10 is our heart's desire: "…*Be **faithful until death**, and I will give you the crown of life*" (NKJV, emphasis added).

We pray that anyone we have hurt in any way, especially our sons and family members, will forgive us. Our heart has always been to walk worthy of the high calling of God in Christ Jesus. However, our humanity is flawed, and we recognize that we are clay in the Master's hands being shaped into vessels He can use for His purposes. Likewise, we release and forgive those who have caused us hurt. The words of the refrain from the hymn "Through It All" (1971) by Andraé Crouch come to mind:

> Through it all, through it all,
> I've learned to trust in Jesus;
> I've learned to trust in God.
> Through it all, through it all,
> I've learned to depend upon his word.2

If my story was a blessing to you, please contact me and let me know. And please share on social media how your friends can obtain a copy of my story. Thank you.

www.linktr.ee/DocMartin
mjaratcliffe@gmail.com
(352) 601-6800

---

2 Andrae Crouch, "Through It All" (CMG Song #1061), Copyright © 1971 Manna Music (ASCAP) (adm. at CapitolCMGPublishing. com) All rights reserved. Used by permission.

SCHOOLS THAT MAKE THE GRADE

BY MARTIN RATCLIFFE

Schools That Make the Grade is written with you, the educator, in mind, whether you are in a K-12 public, private, Christian, or homeschool setting. (The principles even apply at the college level.)

Seven critical success factors that correlate with student academic achievement are discussed. Each success factor is research-based and has explicit implementation strategies for superintendents, principals, and teachers.

In addition to research, stories, perspectives, and case studies, each chapter concludes with discussion questions, making this book ideal for professional development. PowerPoint slides are available at https://linktr.ee/DocMartin. You may switch out picture slides to include pictures of your setting.

ISBN 978-1-59857-090-8
RETAIL $29.95

PURCHASE FROM AMAZON
OR PAUL H BROOKES PUBLISHING CO

www.ingramcontent.com/pod-product-compliance
Lightning Source LLC
Chambersburg PA
CBHW071321120626

46546CB00002B/391